THE
OLD SOMERSET
RAILROAD

A Lifeline for Northern Mainers

Building the Gulf Stream trestle.

THE
OLD SOMERSET
RAILROAD

A Lifeline for Northern Mainers

WALTER M. MACDOUGALL

DOWN EAST BOOKS

CAMDEN, MAINE

Dedication

My thanks to all those who have enriched my life by sharing
their experiences on and along the old Somerset.
To these people this book is dedicated
and especially to the memory of
Eva Bachelder
Reed Hilton
Arthur Tupper
and
Pearl Woodard

Copyright © 2000 by Walter Marshall Macdougall
Book design by Janet Patterson
Printed and bound by Versa Press, Inc.; East Peoria, Illinois

1   3   5   4   2

Down East Books
P.O. Box 679
Camden, ME 04843
BOOK ORDERS: 1-800-685-7962

Library of Congress Cataloging-in-Publication Data

Macdougall, Walter Marshall.
   The old Somerset railroad / by Walter M. Macdougall.
      p. cm.
   ISBN 0-89272-492-7
      1. Somerset Railway. 2. Railroads–Maine. I. Title.

TF25.S62 M32 2000
385'.09741–dc21

99-087562

Contents

A Rough Overview of Events

1861 Somerset Railroad begins legal existence (*page 2*).

1868 Embden approves purchase of Somerset stock (*11*). Maine Central invests $50,000 (*12*). Work begins on roadbed (*11*).

1872 First Somerset rail laid (*2, 11*). Tracks reach Norridgewock (*12*). John Ayer becomes Somerset president (*15*).

1873 National financial panic (*12*). Somerset directors decide to run railroad themselves (*12*).

1874 Somerset authorized to connect with proposed Canadian road (*11*). Joel Gray dies (*12*). Passenger trains begin running into Norridgewock.

1876 Somerset reaches North Anson (*14*). William Ayer joins Somerset (*15*).

1878 Two Somerset stations have telegraph facilities (*16*).

1879 Freshets wash out trestles (*16*).

1881 William Ayer becomes Somerset superintendent (*15*).

1883 Somerset discusses William Atkinson's route to Canada (*16*). Somerset defaults on mortgage for second time (*16*). Reuben Dunn and others bring suit against Somerset on behalf of bondholders. Company reorganized as Somerset Railway (*16*).

1887 New machine shop built at Oakland (*16*). Old Somerset Railroad mortgage foreclosed (*16*). Boston & Quebec challenges Somerset's right to extend to Canada (*18*). Somerset issues $225,000 in bonds and starts laying track for Solon (*19*). Phone lines run from Norridgewock to Madison (*46*).

1888 Embden has completed tracks and station (*13*). Tracks cross Kennebec to reach Solon (*85*).

1889 Somerset builds its first iron bridge.

1890 Somerset reaches Bingham (*4*).

1893 Anson sues Somerset Railway and loses (*17*).

1897 John Ayer no longer Somerset president (*15*). Freshets wash out much trackage (*28*). Phone lines reach North Anson (*46*).

1900 Madison's brick station completed (*30*).

1903 John Fremont Hill becomes Somerset president (*50*).

1904 Somerset sold to Kennebec Valley Railroad Company, name changed to Somerset Railway; construction begins on tracks from Bingham northward to Kineo (*5, 53*). Construction of trestle over Gulf Stream begins (*86*).

1906 Rails completed to Kineo (*50*). On December 3, first train enters Kineo (*52*). Madison bridge burns (*80*).

1907 Passenger service from Bingham to Kineo authorized (*8*). Maine Central issues $1.5 million in bonds, buying control of Somerset (*57*). Wooden bridge at North Anson replaced with an iron one (*83*).

1908 Four men killed in one tragic year (*39*).

1911 Somerset merges with the Maine Central (*59*). George Foster is superintendent (*71*). Pearl Woodard becomes Bingham station master (*73*).

1920 Holman Day novel filmed in Madison (*28*). Murder of Asa Entreken in Embden (*71*).

1929 On March 11, Somerset officially dissolved (*138*).

1933 Service to Kineo ends, Bingham returns to being railhead (*8*).

1936 Crews begin taking up track from Austin Junction northward (*140*).

1945 Pearl Woodard retires (*73*).

PART I

---

*Spiking Down
a Dream*

Boarding a Somerset train at Oakland. The building whose windows
appear behind and above the passenger car housed the railroad's office.
Before 1907, the Somerset enterprise was located above the Dunn Edge
Tool Company office, also in Oakland. AUTHOR'S COLLECTION

Chapter One

∽

THE SOMERSET

THIS IS THE ACCOUNT of a small railway in Maine, but more than that it's a story about people.

For instance, consider a single mile of Somerset track. In straightforward figures this much trackage represents forty-nine tons of rail (a number that would climb as lighter rail was replaced by heavier steel), thirty-five hundred cedar ties, fifty-five or so kegs of spikes, and another twenty tons of rail plates, rail joiners, and bolts, along with yard after yard of ballast. In the 1870s the Somerset was spending an average of thirty thousand dollars to build a mile of track. This price tag included bridges, but it is still a very large figure in those days when molasses cost fifty-five cents a gallon and butter was eighteen cents a pound. All such facts are important, but there is much more to be figured in.

What about the innumerable men who swung an eight-pound spike hammer all day long in the July sun, or who cut the ties and shaped them with broadax and drawshave for thirty-six cents a tie? Then there are the Italian workers who lie in unnamed graves at Bingham. There are the citizens who, dreaming of a new prosperity, voted for their towns to buy stock in the railroad, and there are those few with money and political power who followed their own agendas by promoting the Somerset.

Tracks are for trains and trains are for people, their commerce, and their dreams. The Somerset trains brought the forest down to the mills and hauled away the wood products. For the farmer and the canning companies, they opened new markets. Twice they carried young men off to war. Once, in World War II, after the Somerset had become a branch of the Maine Central, the rails carried German POWs to a work camp in the woods. The trains brought the circus, the mail, the drummers, and the sundry items that the hardware proprietor had promised were "on the iron." They took throngs of people on a day's outing and carried thousands of vacationers to resorts and sporting camps.

In many ways the lives of those who lived along the tracks became interwoven with the railroad. People heard in the whistle of a passing train the long wail of might-have-beens and the resonant call of still-might-bes.

The Somerset was born as one of many schemes for linking the Maine coast with Canadian businesses. Although it never did realize its goal of spanning the miles of mountains and wilderness between Wiscasset and Quebec, its track did finally join with the rails of the Canadian Pacific.

The railroad began its paper existence one month before South Carolina fired on Fort Sumter. Nine hundred and twenty citizens from Embden, North Anson, Madison Bridge (Madison), Solon, North New Portland, and Norridgewock signed a petition to the Maine state legislature pleading for progress and respectfully demanding the right to build a railroad that would connect the signers' villages to prosperity. A charter was granted, but it was 1872 before construction began.

There were to be three periods of growth in the Somerset Railroad's fifty-one years of existence as an independent entity. From 1872 to 1876, through the enthusiasm and tenacity of local promoters, twenty-five miles of rails were laid reaching from Oakland to North Anson. The next extension, sixteen miles, occurred from 1887 through 1890 when the threat of competition forced the railroad to push north to Bingham. In 1904 the last extension was begun—forty-nine and a half miles through the North Woods to Moosehead Lake.

If not in miles then in many other ways, the Somerset ended far from where it started. During the sixty years between the first construction and the Somerset's demise—a managerial takeover by the Maine Central in 1911 that was formalized into a 1924 legal merger—the human world of the upper Kennebec Valley changed in fundamental ways, and the railroad's early problems were largely forgotten except by those who had struggled and lived through the risks.

Railroading remains hazardous work, but when the Somerset first began to run trains the job was positively dangerous. As late as 1898, the railroad commissioners thought it worthy of special note that all the Somerset's engines had recently been fitted with either Eames Vacuum or Westinghouse air brakes, and that all passenger cars had air brakes. Evidently at this late date brakemen were still walking the top of freight cars to set the hand brakes. And years later the old link-and-pin couplings were still being used on log trains. They could be murderous devices; one slip and a trainman could lose his fingers in an instant.

Through the years several ingenious mechanics, under the direction of old Cap Crowell, kept the wheels rolling and conjured up whatever special equipment the road needed. Cap knew each engine and talked to them all as if they had ears with which to listen. The shop crew from Oakland spent hours jacking and coaxing derailed cars back on the track. Later, when the Somerset had extended beyond Bingham, they said a few words under their mustaches when twice a year it came time for the nasty job of converting the engines from coal to oil, or vice versa.

Early on, many employees had to wait for their pay after long hours of hard work. Perhaps there would have been labor troubles if these men hadn't been brought up to expect a life of hard work and little cash in their pockets. Times got better, but still everyone had to pitch in. After a day's passenger run, conductors and brakemen pulled on their overalls and frocks to do the yard switching. Reed Hilton, the chief clerk, remembered when he was called to Rockwood (Kineo Station on Moosehead Lake) to help put engine number 22 back on the rails. The mercury read twenty below, and a blizzard was heaping up three feet of snow. After finishing at Rockwood the crew started back to Oakland–pushing a plow and flanger to clear the line. The plow derailed, and by the time they got that piece of equipment back on the iron they'd been at work for forty-three hours!

The first engines were small 4-4-0s (two driving wheels on each side). They bore such proud old names as the *Carrabassett, Moxie,* and *Messalonskee.* Eight cars made a good train for these locomotives. Engineman Arthur Tupper recalled Superintendent William Ayer saying, "Take all you can pull out with, boys, and double where she stalls." Of course that meant more work for the train crew. "Doubling" involved pulling the pin on half the cars and leaving them behind, to be hauled up the grade after the first half of the train had made the top and been set off on the nearest siding. Later the Somerset got bigger locomotives–ten-wheelers (three driving wheels on each side) designed to haul the heavier freights. This new motive power necessitated ten-foot additions to turntables and engine houses.

The Somerset used its own coaches for local passengers. The oldest cars served to transport the woodsmen who, having spent their wages in wild sprees, had to be herded back to the tall timber under lock and key. In contrast were the Pullmans, which were picked up from the Maine Central at Oakland. After the Somerset had been extended to Moosehead, vacationers could board a car in Boston and not change until they disembarked on the pier at Kineo Station beside the great lake. In those days and for the cost of twenty-five fares, you could reserve a private car and arrive with the hope of causing some stir.

Oakland was the Somerset's home base. There the railroad painted its cars, tinkered with its secondhand engines, and patched its equipment, as well as interchanging freight and passengers with the Maine Central. Beside the Somerset main line as it passed the paint shop in Oakland Yard was a ball signal that indicated when the track was clear for trains heading north. It was an antiquated apparatus, simple and sufficient. A metal ball attached to a rope was raised or lowered on a mast that one old railroader described as a "gallows high enough to hang Haman." With the ball at masthead—a "high ball" in railroad vernacular—trains pulled out of Oakland Yard and made a run for the grade up Otis Hill. At sidings like Hoxie's and Bangs, the train would set off wayfreight. These places were also flag stops where, if the green and white flag was out, passenger or combination trains stopped to pick up people waiting by the tracks. At Bangs was a water tank and a spur to Dodling Quarry. It was an easy downhill grade from Bangs to the beautiful old shire town of Norridgewock on the Kennebec River.

After crossing that river for the first time, the Somerset ran on to Madison. Initially there was no station at Madison; that honor went to Anson (just across the river), which—like the towns of Norridgewock, Embden, and Bingham—had bought stock in the railway. Later, with a booming paper mill, Madison got its depot. Spanning the wide sweep of the Kennebec for a second time, the tracks followed the western bank to North Anson and Embden. Crossing the river for the third time, the railroad reached Solon unheralded by the usual bell ringing and shouting. Like Madison, Solon, always conservative, had turned the railway solicitors away. Again, the Somerset's directors were not about to cut off their noses to spite their faces. Solon was soon to have its station, not to mention a pulp mill, a potato house, and a corn canning factory. In season this plant was surrounded with a village of tents set up by farmers and their families, who had arrived hoping to earn some spending money.

In 1890, having won a court case against its competitors that went all the way to the Supreme Court, the Somerset reached the hill-cradled village of Bingham. On June 12, 1890, Willis Goodrich, Bingham's postmaster and a member of that hamlet's patriarchal family, wrote in his diary: "Four o'clock P.M. The last spike was driven in the railroad. . . . A large crowd went down to see the sight." From the knoll just across the street from where the new depot would stand, the Revere bell in the church rang out the news. From Flagstaff Hill came the boom of the town's cannon. (Luckily, this cannon did not explode—as it was soon to do on an unfortunate Fourth of July. A piece of flying metal hit one Arlie Dinsmore on the head and, to all appearances, killed him. He survived, however, and became the town's undertaker.) The crowd cheered, and there were free cigars—though Deacon Goodrich does not mention this in his diary. Into all

Ballasting the last mile of track into Bingham. A note on the back of the original photograph identified this as the first train to arrive in the village, on June 12, 1890, at 4:10 PM. AUTHOR'S COLLECTION

this excitement came the *Carrabassett* with her cabbage stack and whale-oil head-lamp big as a cyclops's eye.

Bingham's cry had been, "A railroad we must have," and the Somerset had finally arrived. The Rollins brothers, a "bit oiled up," came down from Babbit Ridge for the occasion. As the tumult of welcome for the arriving train subsided, the brothers, arms about each other's shoulders, walked up to the locomotive. "Gosh," said one, "ain't you glad you don't have to steer that thing?"

Perhaps steering should have been a general topic of conversation for those gathered that exciting day in Bingham. How much do we humans steer and how much are we steered by technological progress? More to the immediate point, who was steering the Somerset and with what motives? Certainly those behind the wheel were no longer the original railroad's directors—nor were the small towns that, like Bingham, had bought stock.

For fourteen years Bingham was the Somerset's northern terminus. Then the lure of Canadian business combined with the interests of hotel magnates and owners of vast tracts of woodlands to push the railroad farther north. There was much financial jockeying. During a brief eleven days in 1904, the Somerset Railway was sold to the Kennebec Valley Railroad Company, which then changed its name to the Somerset Railway. With a new bond issue secured by the Maine Central Railroad–an early stockholder in the Somerset–the move north was on.

From Austin Junction just below the Bingham railroad yard, the rails branched to the right and began the climb. Again it was work for dumpcarts, pickaxes, and muscle power. Again came the sound of sledges slamming down on handheld drills and the boom of blasting ledge. The line made its way up the Austin, cutting a notch into the high hillsides overlooking that tumbling stream. Around sharp curves, through rock cuts, and over temporary trestles the railway ran until there was nothing in front of the new roadbed. The line had reached a steep valley running at right angles to its path. Here the rails took to the air on a slender trestle 500 feet long and a dizzying 125 feet above a cascading flow of white water and dark pools called Gulf Stream. "The Trestle" was to become a saga in its own right.

Eight miles from Bingham and nine hundred feet higher in elevation, the trains reached Deadwater, their engine tanks in need of water and the fireman deserving of whatever rest he could get. When I was a boy the rails were gone, and Deadwater was primarily a large sawdust pile. The water spout banged in the wind against its empty tank; the station was lifeless. Though I could still buy a candy bar in the old store, Deadwater seemed a lonely place–flat, open to the sun, and filled with the white-crowned sparrows' plaintive song.

But in the time when the engines took on water and trains made their "meets" here there'd been a school, a post office, and lots of goods on display behind the store's plate-glass windows. It was sometimes even an exciting place, as when a movie crew arrived to film one of Holman Day's novels and used Walter Robinson's logging camp as an authentic set.

Beyond Deadwater the railroad entered the lumber kingdom. Mile after mile the Somerset snaked its way through the forested hills, its two rails flanked by tall fir and spruce. A few miles above Deadwater at Bald Mountain Station, a spur ran east to Austin Lake and northward to Bald Mountain Pond and the timber waiting there.

Continuing on its way to its junction with the Canadian Pacific, the Somerset skirted Moxie Pond and ran to Forsythe, where the whining saws of the Skinner mill did their part in converting a forest into boards. At Indian Pond another group of camps clustered about the depot. During the spring log drives, men swarmed in.

Deadwater Station, looking south. In late afternoon, the village awaits
the cool of evening and the ceasing of the saw's whine.
AUTHOR'S COLLECTION

The station at Rockwood, on Moosehead Lake, the Somerset's terminus.
The wharf, depot, freight shed, and 200' of canopy cost a total of $6,982.
ROBERT LORD COLLECTION

They swung down from the coach steps with their calk studded boots tied by the laces and slung around their necks. In winter the station platform was piled with grain for the horses and new recruits for the lumber operations.

The flag stop for Mike Marr's sporting camps came next, and then, at last, the meeting with the Canadian Pacific rails at Somerset Junction. There was something of the frontier about this place. It had a tough reputation, especially when the hotel was full of loggers—which was often.

Six miles more and the railway reached what was to be its final destination. Once a passenger on a Somerset train who had been pestering the conductor with questions asked if he were sure the train stopped at Rockwood.

"If it don't," the conductor answered, "there's going to be one hell of a splash!"

At Rockwood the rails ran out onto a long pier surrounded by Moosehead Lake on three sides. The Somerset brought tons of supplies and carloads of loggers bound for the camps of the north. Julian Estes, who was the station agent at

The Somerset's mechanic shop (with the chimney) and blacksmith shop, at the railroad's home base in Oakland. AUTHOR'S COLLECTION

Kineo Station (Rockwood) for years, remembered the morning when he sold three hundred dollars worth of tickets to outgoing lumberjacks.

Summer brought a different clientele. Moosehead, that great "queen of inland lakes," shrinks to three quarters of a mile wide at Rockwood. Directly across the "narrows" and below the spectacular felcite cliffs of Mount Kineo stood a five-story hotel. It was a part of the Ricker Hotel empire—electric lights, Oriental rugs, elevators, a golf course, a marina. The Kineo House was billed as the "largest and most luxurious inland water hotel in America." At the railway depot porters piled trunks and bags under the long awning, which ran the length of the platform. The sleek hulls of steamboats, with names like the *Marguerite* (which met the first train into Rockwood) and the *Priscilla* (which met the last), eased up to the slips along the roofed pier. At night the lights of the "Big House" glittered from across the lake, and the strains of a band drifted over the water.

On any evening, be it in the soft after-warmth of a summer day or in the blue shadows of winter drifts, the ruby red and the yellow-green of switch lanterns marked the railway's single track north through the villages and farms of the upper Kennebec. From Bingham on, the lanterns glowed between the dark walls of the woods. Perhaps never again will travel be more convenient, mails more regular, or transportation more efficient.

Passenger service from Bingham to Kineo had been authorized in 1907. Twenty-six years later, and after an expenditure of some $1.6 million to build the extension, the last train order governing traffic between Bingham and Kineo clicked over the telegraph. One employee said it reminded him of a fellow's comment on losing his life's savings on a horse at the North Anson Fair: "Easy come, easy go." Again Bingham became the railhead, and the line settled down to freight service. It was no longer the Somerset Railway, nor the "Kineo Short Line," but simply a branch of the Maine Central.

In the sixty years since the first trains pulled out of Oakland there had been some fine railroading and a great deal of living, but major changes had ushered in a drastically altered way of life. What follows is a story of the Somerset told as near to the recollections of those who lived these times as possible.

**Great expectations: Three young chums look out from a past in which
a watch and a derby hat were objects of pride.**

PAMELA DUNPHY COLLECTION

Chapter Two

SCHEMES

WILLIAM ATKINSON SAT in his Neolithic chair atop a large pile of stones that had been cleared from his hilltop pasture. It was a one-man-made chair, painstakingly constructed and with as much comfort as smooth stones could provide. There was no need for additional sitting room, for Atkinson was a prophet, and so he sat alone. The year was 1868.

Atkinson was a thinker and a dreamer. He had taught school for a term or two until his pedagogical career ended in a row and a lawsuit over his salary—twenty-seven dollars. He did not teach again. Instead he farmed, solved algebraic problems as a pastime, memorized yards of poetry, and became possessed by the vision of an international railroad.

From his chair Bill Atkinson looked across Embden Lake onto range after range of blue mountains. Beyond those mountains was Canada, and these are his own words:

"Our desire is to connect the beautiful Kennebec Valley and all its thriving towns and manufacturing villages, the capital of the state, Augusta, and the unsurpassed deep-sea harbor of Wiscasset, Maine with the Quebec Central Railway and the city of Quebec."

The Somerset was a link in Atkinson's grand plan. Once Oakland had been connected to Wiscasset by rail and the Somerset had been completed to North Anson, then Atkinson's "Carrabassett & Canadian Railway" would swing north and west from that village to cross the border, reach Lake Megantic, and join with its Canadian counterpart. Atkinson may have had a "piping voice," as one local historian reports, but he became eloquent when he talked railroads, and his route was the best of the many proposals for Canadian rail links being championed. Relatively speaking, its grades were not steep; its route was also 440 miles shorter than the distance from Quebec to the Atlantic Ocean at Halifax.

While Atkinson went about his calling as a railroad prophet, his neighbors in Embden were about to get themselves into real trouble assisting the Somerset's construction. There was a feeling of new beginnings in the spring of 1868. Eli Walker, Embden's town constable, tacked the warrant for a special town meeting upon the nail-pocked door of the Town House. A week in advance several well-dressed "out-of-towners" arrived to talk up the proposition of lending money to the railroad. Perhaps they were gifted, or maybe it was simply time for new hope and expectations. On March 28 the Town House was crowded. William Atkinson was sworn in as moderator. Again the well-dressed men spoke.

They realized that Embden was not a rich town and that the forty thousand dollars sought by the railroad was a large sum, but the way to prosperity was as plain as the nose on townfolks' faces. The irresistible appeal lay in the scheme's simplicity. The town would issue bonds and, with the money raised, buy Somerset stock. Embden would have forty years to repay the bonds, but long before this the taxes from increased business and dividends from the stock would have allowed a more rapid payment of the town's incurred debts. The next generation would retire the bonds, thankful that their predecessors had brought them improved opportunities and lifestyles. Finally, considering the certain success of the Somerset, the town would be left part owner of the very instrument that had brought its success.

A remarkable event was taking place in this packed town meeting. The Egyptian symbol for a million is a man with his hands outstretched as if in astonishment. For a farmer or a villager living along the Kennebec in the mid-1800s, this symbol would have been appropriate for a mere thousand dollars. William Atkinson's presence created excitement, and the fact that Joel Gray, perhaps Embden's best-known citizen, was president of the Somerset gave confidence to cautious hearts. But most of all there was a sense of history. Here was the opportunity to be inserted into what Tennyson described as "the ringing groves of change."

The vote was taken: 132 in favor and 7 nays!

In hindsight—of which there was soon to be an abundance—the voters might have insisted on convertible bonds, which would give the bondholders some recompense other than the town's property should things go bad. Someone might have drawn attention to the clause in the Somerset Charter that gave the railroad the right to assess stockholders for construction costs. Unless it was the seven who voted against raising money for the Somerset, no one seems to have figured out that the 7 1/2 percent interest on the bonds would be three thousand dollars—five times what the town was paying for education. And there was another interesting stipulation. The town promised not to sell its bonds until citizens had a chance to buy stock in the railroad. Once this period was over, stock sales to Embden citizens would be closed—with the exception of Joel Gray, who was, after all, president of the railroad.

Four years later, on October 29, 1872, the Somerset began laying rail. The Portland Rolling Mill supplied rail at the rate of forty-five tons per week. The rail crew under W. C. Pitman, Esquire, of Bangor was laying half a mile per day. In November the *General Veazie,* an old engine borrowed from the Maine Central, was pulling and pushing the construction train, and track was in place halfway to Norridgewock. Out in front Messieurs S. G. Mills & Company were grading and setting the masonry for bridges all the way to Madison. Pitman had a crew of ninety men ballasting the new line. A local newspaper commented: "We are glad that this looks like business and more like having a railroad than anything we have seen."

Anticipation was high. The Somerset had already renewed its charter twice and amended it four times. Before a spike was driven, the railroad was authorized to extend to Bingham, that much closer to Canada. By 1874 it was authorized to connect with a proposed Canadian road to be called the "Levis & Kennebec." Behind it all, for those who needed assurance, was the interest of the Maine Central. Joel Gray had been active in the formation of this growing railroad, and the Maine Central's president, Reuben Dunn, was a director of the Somerset. The same year Embden voted to buy stock, the Maine Central invested fifty thousand dollars in the new railroad, thus assuring that it would locate its home base in Oakland and serve as a feeder to the Maine Central's traffic.

The Somerset's track had just reached Norridgewock when the financial panic of 1873 dumped the fires from under the boilers of railroad schemes all across the country. According to the *Bangor Whig and Courier,* the Somerset's directors had decided to run the railroad themselves despite "flattering offers." It's hard to imagine from whom those offers might have come. The Maine Central was under the thumb of the Eastern Railroad, which sent its superintendent to look at the little Somerset, but nothing came of this visit. It was rumored that the Boston & Maine, the Eastern's archenemy, might lease the Somerset, but again nothing materialized.

Back in Embden, Eli Walker hardly had time to tear down one warrant for a special town meeting before there was another to take its place. In less than a month the town met three times. It voted first not to issue the remaining town bonds, then to rescind the first vote, and finally to stop the bond issuance. And now the citizens of Embden faced a new problem. The railroad's charter gave it the right to sell off any stockholders' certificates if they did not pay construction cost assessments. Embden voters quickly voted to issue the remainder of the bonds if the railroad would stop selling the town's railroad stock.

There was talk of new mills at Madison and excitement at Anson, but for the towns that had voted to help the Somerset and still had no railroad, the mood was solemn if not downright sour. There was irony, too. In 1874 Embden's Joel Gray died in Boston. His remains were brought home as far as the rails went, which was six miles short of North Anson and several more from Embden. Gray's neighbors met the train at the railhead and conveyed his body home. By 1877, eleven years before Embden would get its railroad and station, forty-four farms (20 percent of all the farms) had been sold for back taxes.

Then Embden voted not to pay the interest on its bonds, and the fat was in the fire. Rumors spread that the bondholders would attach private property. Cattle were moved to neighboring towns, and farms were deeded over to relatives who lived in other communities. The rumors quickly became fact. The bondholders chose to attach the most prosperous farm in Embden, which belonged to one George L. Eames, and Deputy Sheriff Clap duly served the lien. Eames sued the bondholders for "wrongful execution" and charged the sheriff with trespass. The only happy ones were the lawyers.

The case involved private property and public obligation. The three lawyers for the plaintiff brought forth a ream of legal precedence reaching back to Edward I, bolstered by the Fourteenth Amendment and the sixth article of the Maine Bill of Rights. *Bondholders v. Town of Embden* was a test case—that much everyone knew. Bingham, which had voted to raise ten thousand dollars to buy Somerset stock, had a similar case pending in the County Court at Skowhegan, and the town of Anson was watching for the results.

The *Somerset Reporter,* the county's leading newspaper, made its own observations. Embden would have to pay it debts or no town in the state would be able to raise a dollar through the sale of bonds. The Maine high court's verdict (1886) was in favor of the bondholders. A small group of men took on the task of getting Embden's shambled house back in order. Thad Boothby, the town treasurer, volunteered to collect back taxes, riding on horseback from farm to farm and returning home late at night. In the darkness the roads he traveled were little more than narrow notches between the bushes. Everyone in town knew that Boothby carried money, and each night his family worried until they heard the clip of his horse's shoes on the gravel drive. No harm came to Boothby, but concerns were doubtlessly well founded.

Norridgewock Station. Carts full of corn wait to be unloaded at the Burnham and Morrill canning factory. ROBERT LORD COLLECTION

Others came forward to help. Andrew Libby—Somerset director, president of the National Bank, and Embden farm owner—loaned his own money and got the best terms he could for loans to the town. You can't get blood out of a turnip, they told the bondholders. At first the town voted to pay thirty-seven cents on the dollar, then fifty cents. By 1890 the debt was paid. Norridgewock, Anson, Concord, and Bingham all met their debts as best they could.

Meanwhile the Somerset, for all its financial difficulties, was inching northward. By 1872 it had reached Norridgewock. The center of the village migrated south across the Kennebec River and clustered around the new depot. The year 1876 saw the Somerset cross the Kennebec for a second time and establish a new railhead on the southern bank of the Carrabassett River at North Anson. Business was improving slowly. The railroad commissioners reported that road and bridge work were generally good, and the railroad was well managed. Two hundred and twenty-four passenger trains, 112 freight trains, and 625 mixed trains were run that year, carrying an average of fourteen passengers and fifteen tons of freight each.

Every town along the Somerset's rails and along its proposed route north-ward had its cadre of railroad enthusiasts, and occasionally this support rose to the level of unselfish devotion. Edwin Rowe, for example, was judge probate for the county and had made his money toting goods from Skowhegan to Norridge-wock. A railroad would put an end to this traffic, yet Rowe was an avid advocate for the Somerset. He became a director and treasurer of the road and helped out on the trains themselves. Coupling the cars with link and pin was a treacherous job even for professional railroaders, and Judge Rowe one day got jammed between two cars while helping to make up a train in Norridgewock. The newspaper said there was little hope for this sixty-year-old, but he survived, and in his last days his grateful town furnished him with a home and housekeeper.

While each town produced its share of railroad supporters, Oakland fur-nished the triumvirate that was to become the backbone of the Somerset's orga-nization. Their names were Reuben Dunn, John Ayer, and Major Abner Small.

Dunn owned Oakland's major industry, the Dunn Edge Tool Company. Powered by Messalonskee Stream, his factory turned out ten thousand dozen

(Left) John Ayer, president of the Somerset from 1872 to 1897.
(Right) Abner R. Small, a Civil War hero and treasurer of the Somerset until 1915.
OAKLAND HISTORICAL SOCIETY

axes and fifteen thousand scythes annually. He brought the experience of being president of the Maine Central to the Somerset, along with a business sense as sharp as the tools that bore his name.

If Dunn had any weakness, it was for butter. In an unpublished journal, John Ayer's son (another John) has left us an image of Dunn seated at the Ayer's dining room table. Swathed in a large napkin that is clipped around his neck, he is eating cut slices of butter with his fingers. For young John, strictly trained by his mother in table manners, it was an amazing spectacle.

John Ayer, senior, was a close friend and business partner of Reuben Dunn. When Ayer returned to Oakland after a railroad surveying in the Midwest, he became a treasurer of Dunn Edge Tool. Together Ayer and Dunn built the Cascade Woolen Mills in Oakland and planned for textile mills in Madison as soon as the railroad got that far. In 1872 Ayer became president of the Somerset, a position he was to hold for twenty-five years.

Again, young John Ayer's journal gives us a glimpse of those years when his father was president of the Somerset. The elder Ayer would take the boy up to the railroad's shop and have an engine brought from the roundhouse. Then they would go up the line to check on the supply of firewood for the locomotives or maybe to inspect the repairs being made on a bridge. John looked back on those trips as the times he really got to know his father.

Young John Ayer was fourteen when his father died. The railroad cars were draped in black crepe, and his father's body was borne from the church to Oakland's lakeside cemetery between lines of mill employees and Somerset men.

Major Abner Small was treasurer of the Cascade Woolen Mills and soon became treasurer of the Somerset and clerk of the corporation. His mild appearance—above and below a tremendous mustache—belied his determination and experience. Starting as a sergeant in the hard-hitting and hard-hit Sixteenth Regiment of Maine volunteers, Small had risen to a field commission of major in the Civil War. He had been taken prisoner but had survived the ordeal unscathed. At the close of the war, he led his regiment in the Grand Review.

In the same year that the Somerset reached North Anson, John Ayer's son, William, joined the small force at the Somerset's office on Dunn Street in Oakland. Like his father he was a practical surveyor, having attended Dean Academy and Westbrook Seminary. Bill had worked laying out the roadbed from Madison to North Anson. He became the general ticket agent and, in 1881, superintendent of the Somerset. He wore a lot of other hats besides: senior member of Ayer & Greeley Coal Company (Horace Greeley was the Somerset's accountant), superintendent of the Dunn Edge Tool Company, treasurer of the Dodling Granite Quarry (a contributor to the Somerset's freight traffic), president of the Oakland Woolen Mills, and a director of the Madison Woolen Company. Someway he found time to serve as a representative to the state legislature, an active Free Mason, and a lieutenant colonel on the staff of Governor John Fremont Hill (who was later to be a prominent player in the final extension of the Somerset to Moosehead Lake). Moreover, Bill Ayer managed to show up along the Somerset wherever he was least expected. He was respected and liked by many of the railroad's employees–not an easy feat sometimes. Finally, Bill Ayer was of Yankee as well as Scottish descent when it came to money. When the Dodling quarry was abandoned, for instance, Bill sent a crew to dismantle the buildings and take down the derrick mast, which he wanted sawed into lumber; from what was saved, he built several houses in Oakland that he rented. He even wanted the chimneys taken down brick by brick, but the foreman toppled them when the boss wasn't around. It took careful men like Bill Ayer to keep the Somerset going.

William M. Ayer, the longtime superintendent of the Somerset Railroad.
AUTHOR'S COLLECTION

Despite the financial problems, the Somerset not only survived but managed to constantly improve its equipment, tracks, and services. Bit by bit iron rail was replaced with steel, and the old rail was used in constructing short-span bridges. A contrivance allowed the track crew to clear ditches, which were always a problem, with a water jet. Wooden trestles–both those put in when the road was first constructed and those necessitated by washouts in the 1879 freshets–were replaced by stone culverts and fill. By 1878 two stations had telegraph facilities. Coaches were repainted inside and out, and baggage cars rebuilt. In 1887 a new machine shop was built at Oakland. It all added up to good railroading, and the railroad commissioners repeatedly commended the Somerset for its ingenuity, its safe and efficient operation, and the good repair of its rolling stock.

In 1883, the same year in which the Somerset was talking about using Atkinson's route up the Carrabassett to Canada, the railroad defaulted on its mortgage for the second time. Something had to be done. The Oakland leadership took a bold step. Reuben Dunn (who held Somerset bonds), acting for the other bondholders, brought suit against the railroad. A new company, the Somerset Railway, was formed and bought the old railroad at public auction. In 1887 the old Somerset Railroad mortgage was foreclosed.

Most of the bondholders in the old railroad were persuaded to exchange their bonds for stock in the new railway at some percentage of the original face value. The engines kept trailing their smoke along the Kennebec. John Ayer was president of the new company, and his son was superintendent.

Ten years after the formation of the new railway the town of Anson, along with several other private bondholders in the original railroad, became aware that the Somerset was no longer their company. Their bonds, though still a debt of the new company, were not secured by the original mortgage of the railroad. They brought suit against the Somerset Railway Company. D. D. Stewart, who by this time had become an old standby in Somerset-related litigations, headed the team of lawyers for the plaintiffs. Anson claimed that it had never authorized its town fathers to use its bonds in the formation of the new company. The town's lawyers argued that no person's property can be transferred by an act of legislature. In the end the court ruled that these objections came too late; the legal term is *estople by laches,* which in everyday parlance means that the plaintiff waited too long before trying to shut the door. The Somerset Railway was securely legal.

There were those who felt that the Oakland management had looked after its own interests and the towns had been squeezed out. Perhaps the people in

Embden were the most bitter. Historian Pamela Dunphy tells a story that reveals the depth of their anger. On hearing the train whistle, one Embdenite would always exclaim, "That goddamn train ruined this town."

Whatever truth there may be in such assertions, for all their efforts the towns had been a small part of the financial picture. The costs for construction and equipment during the period of extension from Oakland to Bingham totaled $1,068,758. Even assuming the maximum that the towns promised to raise, their part would only represent 22 percent. In financial terms it was never more than a quarter truth that the Somerset was their railroad, but quarter truths often serve progress and the welfare of communities quite well. This feeling of proprietorship remained among the townspeople along the Somerset. In 1900 a Madison newspaper observed: "It has been many years since *our* railroad has been so completely blocked by snow and ice" (emphasis added).

Four years after the formation of the new Somerset Railway came the first real challenge to the Somerset's long-held right to extend to Bingham and northward. As someone once said about the Great Depression, it wouldn't have been so bad if it hadn't happened at such a bad time. The challenger was another Maine-to-Canada scheme, the Boston & Quebec Airline Railroad, which would leave Skowhegan and run up the Kennebec Valley to join with the Canadian Pacific.

To clarify the picture, Skowhegan was the railhead for a Maine Central branch line that had never figured in the Somerset's plans. True, there had been a survey for a two-foot-gauge connection between the Somerset at Norridgewock and Skowhegan and on to Athens. That survey line ran through a number of barns, whose owners were relieved when this scheme did not materialize. One farmer said that he would be damned if he'd go out and open his barn doors every time the cars wanted to go through.

There was no joking at the Somerset's Oakland office when the news broke of this competing venture. Big guns were behind the Skowhegan initiative, including ex-governor Abner Coburn, who had been president of the Maine Central when, early on, it lost interest in leasing the Somerset. Coburn was a Skowhegan man, through whose influence Skowhegan had wrested the county seat from Norridgewock. His interests, however, ranged in many directions; he held vast timber holdings in the upper Kennebec region and owned steamboats on Moosehead Lake.

Worrisome as well to Somerset supporters was the route that Coburn and his associates were proposing. It sounded all too feasible. Only one major bridge and a long trestle at a place called the Forks, not much ledge to blast, and no curves tighter than eight degrees. Of chief concern for the Somerset's lawyers was the plaintiffs' contention that the Somerset was blocking the development of international commerce. The railroad had lain back too long, content with its railhead at North Anson, and thereby lost its exclusive right to extend northward.

The hearing at the courthouse in Skowhegan was packed. The Somerset objected strongly to the upstart's contentions. If it had not extended north, it certainly intended to do so; moreover, it had its chartered right to extend "by the most feasible route through the town of Moscow and the plantations to Canada." The commissioners at the hearing were faced with a difficult and politically loaded decision but escaped through a technicality: Before they could rule, a complete survey of the new road would have to be presented. It was a victory of sorts for the Somerset. It was also a clear signal that the company had to cross the Carrabassett and start laying track for Solon.

The Somerset issued another $225,000 worth of bonds and the railroad was again on the move.

The prospering town of Madison. The Weston House is visible to the right, and the Madison Woolen Mill is on the left. The tracks inside the long, covered railroad bridge cross the Kennebec and lead to Anson, still a country village despite the financial backing it received from the Somerset.

Chapter Three

ALONG THE RAILS TO BINGHAM

At Oakland the Somerset shared a passenger station with the Maine Central. When it rained, passengers could keep dry under the gingerbread-fringed canopy until it was time to board the Somerset train. Then both passengers and the baggage wagon had to cross the planking laid between the rails of the Maine Central's main line. Hauling a loaded wagon across the planks was a job more suited for a horse than a man. Often two hundred pieces of baggage had to be transferred between trains–trunks, cases, boxes, and the like.

The two roads also shared the sorting yard below the depot, but that yard was definitely Maine Central turf. The bigger road guarded its territory with a ball signal that forbad the Somerset engines–unless a sphere and a red lantern were at the masthead–from passing beyond their own yard limit. Even with a favorable signal, enginemen were required to make a full stop before crossing or entering Maine Central tracks. (Incidentally, if the use of *red* as a go-ahead signal seems strange, think about that famous freight line the Red Ball Express.)

Some precaution was necessary, but it was no secret that the Maine Central's brass considered the Somerset's country-bred operation a threat. Men who worked on both roads claimed that the Somerset had nothing to be ashamed of– an opinion shared by the state railroad commissioners. The Maine Central management remained unconvinced. They pointed to the occasion when a car of dynamite had gotten away and every man on the Somerset crew (which was doing the switching) ran for cover. Then there was that affair with engine number 6–the "Old Lady," as everyone around the Somerset's shop called her.

The car foreman had wanted a few cars moved, and the Somerset's superintendent had elected to do the job himself. Before picking up the cars, the superintendent stopped at the paint shop to run another errand, leaving number 6 without pinning the throttle. Under back pressure the throttle opened a notch, and the Old Lady took off up the main line toward Norridgewock. A message was hammered north on the telegraph in an attempt to warn a freight train that was working its way toward Oakland. Before the warning could be completed, however, someone yelled out that the Old Lady was returning. It's a hard grade out of Oakland, and number 6 had gone as far she could before running low on steam and yielding to gravity. Just why no one got to the switch and put the engine into the Somerset's own yard was hard to explain, but no one did. The Old Lady piled into a boxcar in Maine Central territory.

It was true that wayfreights experienced too frequent hotboxes which caused delays beside good fishing holes. (The journals on railroad cars' wheels were packed in lubricant-saturated waste. If the journals overheated for any reason, this waste could ignite. One of the purposes of the cupola on cabooses was to give the rear-end crew a chance to watch for these "hotboxes.") It was also true that the Somerset had a special tolerance for characters. But aside from a few who drank too much, the Somerset men were good railroaders. Arthur Tupper, for instance, was a Christian gentleman who could repeat yards of Sir Walter Scott's poems and get the most out of an engine. Once when Tupper was at the throttle of high-wheeled number 12 and pulling the superintendent's special car, William Ayer told him that he wanted to go forty miles per hour. There were no speedometers in locomotive cabs, but Ayer had one in his car. Later, Ayer told Tupper that the needle had moved very little from that mark, and the ride over the line had been like silk. Considering the ups and downs on the Somerset, that was a feat.

I do have to admit that one group of young fellows who worked for the Somerset was usually up to some stunt. Reed Hilton was a member of the gang that painted the lady on the side of the Somerset's tank house in Oakland. The figure was a nice piece of work, fit for any bar in the country except for her large size. In full view of both the Somerset and the Maine Central's main line, she received prompt attention, and the artists were quickly sent back down to the tank with a pail of regulation paint. But Reed Hilton, apart from his pranks, already knew the line and most of the jobs that needed to be done on the Somerset.

The little road got its share of itinerant trainmen or "boomers," as they were called. Most turned out to be good railroaders. However, an investment of a few dollars bought you an impressive pile of fake passes and phony recommendations back then, and Boomer Mooney came to Oakland with a full set. He

Reed Hilton is second from the right in this Maine Central crew. Others include (from left to right) car checker Al Town; brakeman J. Levine, who was later killed when he slipped from the front of an engine; Bert Town; Dave Goodnue; fireman William Dorge, who was killed during the war in France shortly before the armistice; engineer Frank McCrum; and conductor Gid Gulifer. AUTHOR'S COLLECTION

drew his switch key, borrowed a seventeen-jewel watch, and went to work. His work was good, and he soon married a local girl who promptly became pregnant. No one fully realized how resourceful Mooney was until *two* wives appeared at the paymaster's window to collect his pay. Judge Bryant ordered Mooney held for bigamy, and the sheriff locked the man up to await trial. During the night the prisoner escaped and disappeared, never to be found again. No one was surprised. Any man who can keep two wives separated in a town like Oakland has to be capable.

The Somerset's yard and home base was located a quarter mile north of Oakland Station and on the western side of its own track. Over the years a cluster of gray-painted buildings was constructed and enlarged until it included a blacksmith's shop, a heating plant (with an old locomotive boiler), paint and car shops, a mechanic's shop, and several sheds filled with new and old parts. When the switch was made from wood to coal in the early 1900s, the loading crane and its tubs for fueling the engines, along with a coal shed, were added just north of the shops.

Behind the coal shed Skillings' Brook ran through a patch of gray birch before making its way along the edge of the encroaching ash dump and then under the track. It was a scrubby, nondescript location, but even such places along the old Somerset had their stories–humorous or tragic but always human.

Filling the coal tubs at the fueling crane was one of the jobs assigned to Milo Thomas. Milo was a moderate man, and no one was overly surprised at the amount of time he spent at this task. It turned out, however, that his lengthy stays up at the coal yard were directly associated with one of the engine house keepers going partly blind. Dr. Holmes suspected that rawhide booze was the cause of the calamity, and began looking for the source. A likely candidate was the barrel of denatured alcohol kept at the shops to be mixed with kerosene for wiping around the engines. Old Cap Crowell, the mechanical wizard who kept the wheels rolling on the Somerset, assured the doctor that he had discovered long ago that if he mixed all the alcohol with kerosene the moment it arrived, it lasted a lot longer. Then another patient came to Holmes with alarming symptoms and, in his fear, told all. Constable Bert Hersom found Milo at work at his still in the birches behind the coal shed and dumped the produce into Skillings' Brook. Milo was sent downriver for another hitch.

Just across Skillings' Brook was Lady Bug's hut. Lady Bug wore men's pants. Lots of people said she was crazy, but she was too smart to have ever visited Milo Thomas's still. She used the Somerset's track as her personal road to town, and she was going that way when the down passenger train nudged up behind her. Engineman Ross Baker laid on the whistle, and Lady Bug responded with profanity that could have singed a boiler plate. They came into Oakland Station with Lady Bug walking no faster than usual and Ross still blowing the whistle.

A few years later, when no one had seen Lady Bug walking past the machine shop for several days, someone went to check and found her dead in her hut beside the ash dump and Skillings' Brook.

Any engineman who didn't have his train rolling by the time he crossed Skillings' Brook knew that he was in trouble. Freight trains with any tonnage at all used to back down what was known as the racetrack to get a run for the grade out of Oakland. The grade began with Ten Lots Hill and then with only a slight sag, nicknamed Bull Run, climbed Otis Hill. This hill was what railroaders call a "commanding grade," or the hardest to climb on a particular section of track, which thus determines what trains can haul without either double heading or hauling over in separate sections.

For one engineman, Otis Hill was the final straw. His nickname was "Tiger" and that handle will suffice. It was Tiger who ran over two torpedoes (small explosive devices set on the rail to signal an engineer of trouble ahead) and left rear brakeman Reed Hilton waving his flag beside the track. Passing Reed with a cherry-red smile, Tiger slammed into the rear of the train that Reed was trying to protect. Tiger also had the dubious honor of running not only right past a waiting and astonished group on the platform of Oakland Station but straight out onto the Maine Central's main line. Usually his crewmates covered for Tiger when he was drinking, but they could hardly have done so this time. Still, Tiger lived a charmed life until he stalled his train on Otis Hill. The conductor came forward, already hot under his collar at the thought of having to divide his train and double over the hill. And there was Tiger, satchel in hand, climbing down from the engine cab.

"Where are you going?" the conductor asked, laying his hand on Tiger's shoulder.

"If I've got to run an engine that's so damned slow it can't get over Otis Hill then I'm walking." Tiger lurched off up the track and out of the annals of the Somerset.

It's interesting how many of the Somerset's stories take place on grades and tough places rather than the easy flats. Perhaps that's the way with life, too.

Bull Run, officially known as Watsons on the timetable, besides being a sag in the track, had a road crossing and fifteen-car siding. Apart from the obvious associations with the famous battle, Bull Run got its name from George Bull, who lived just east of the road crossing. It was George who put the stuffed deer out under an apple tree as a decoy. He was smart enough to choose a place some distance from his house, for every year the stuffed deer lost more sawdust via another hole or two.

Bill McCloud spotted the deer on his first run as a brakeman. When he was told by the crew that a deer was nearly always seen under that same tree, he got excited and borrowed a rifle. And the next time his train pulled through Bull Run, there sure enough was the deer. The train was short that day, and Ross Baker obligingly stopped. The fireman was doubled up over his shovel and laughing into the fire door while Bill banged away. After a while the crew went down to look. The stuffed deer hadn't lost any more sawdust, but George Bull's plug sorrel was dead. That ended the joke. As soon as he could, Bill went up to

Arthur Cann, a partner in Reed Hilton's nocturnal adventures, rides a "three wheeler" on the tracks just south of the Dodlin Quarry spur.
AUTHOR'S COLLECTION

George Bull's farm and paid him forty-five dollars. The crew got to feeling guilty and chipped in.

Pumping a handcar up the grade out of Oakland was something a man would do only for pay or when he had a date to meet a girl in Norridgewock. One night Reed Hilton and a friend were returning on a "borrowed" pumpcar from such an excursion. They had toiled through the darkness on the uphill grade and were enjoying the ride down Ten Lots Hill. The Somerset in those days was pretty much a daytime affair, so the men were surprised when a light ahead proved that someone else was using the rails. They jumped. Down the track, a pumpcar loaded with an Italian track crew was laboring back from a night on the town of Oakland. There was a moment of surprised faces in the lantern light before the abandoned car slammed into their vehicle and sent them tumbling into the bushes.

Ten Lots Hill cost the Somerset a considerable sum in pumpcars. One afternoon when the grasshoppers were singing their August hot song, George Bull's young sons found a pumpcar sitting on a pullout by the track. The usual chain through the wheel spokes and padlock were missing, so the boys appropriated it. They pumped up the sag to the top of the grade down to Oakland. There the older brother announced that they would just let the car run. Soon the handles began to take on a life of their own, and then they began whacking up and down as the car picked up speed.

"She's gone," the younger boy yelled, and they jumped.

In Oakland, meantime, old number 6 sat on the Somerset's main line. The fireman had gone for a jug of water and Ed Coburn, the engineman, had dozed off with his pipe drooping over his lower lip. The runaway pumpcar slammed into the rear of number 6, shearing off the brake line and setting the brakes on the engine with a rush of air that added to the commotion of splintering wood and clanging iron. Ed jumped up and bit off the stem of his T.D. pipe.

The night of the colliding pumpcars, Reed Hilton and his buddy were returning from the Pines in Norridgewock. Strings of Japanese lanterns lighted the pavilion at the Pines, and the dance music floated out over the Kennebec. People came from all over, which was just what the owners of the electric trolley line from Skowhegan to Norridgewock had hoped would happen. It was good for the Somerset as well. The railroad ran excursions from time to time. For a while and as an incentive, it cost more to come down the line to Madison than it did to Norridgewock.

Upon the arrival of the first trains in Norridgewock, the *Somerset Reporter* observed that the "staid, old town" received "quite a stir." I probably should include the Pines as a somewhat delayed aspect of this "stir." Certainly I could include the Burnham & Morrill corn canning factory, which sat close to the tracks, and the fact that even before the depot was built an enterprising potato buyer from Lewiston had set up headquarters in a boxcar. It was reported that he was going to build a potato house with room for two stores. A local granite quarry produced a fine, dark stone that polished well; that industry would grow as well. Yet the *Colby Atlas* of 1893 shows that the railroad never turned Norridgewock (as it would Madison) into a mill town. Norridgewock was a center for a farming area. Freight trains were soon carrying large quantities of potatoes and hay. Norridgewock remained Norridgewock—a solid if not staid community set in one of the loveliest parts of rural Maine. (It is tempting to view Norridgewock as a village of virtue on a peaceful sweep of the Kennebec. Still, in October 1875 Dr. Brown of that town was waylaid while riding through a patch of woods. He got away by using his whip. As he dashed off, his assailant took a shot at him. Two years later, a temperance advocate left the village with a friend's watch and a bunch of unpaid bills.)

In 1877 the railroad commissioners' report made a big deal of the historic and scenic country through which the Somerset was building its tracks. Ninety-five years before rails were laid along the upper Kennebec, Benedict Arnold's men on their way to storm Quebec had marveled at this country of river and rolling hills. "A garden of the gods," one man described it in his journal. Captain Farrar, in his *Illustrated Guide Book to Moosehead,* encouraged travelers to take note of the "vistas" to be seen from the Somerset coach windows as the trains rounded the curves along the Kennebec. Indeed, after this trip passengers remembered the sweeps of river reflecting sky, cloud, and the dark and sunlit greens of woods and fields–a hundred pastoral images, like the brick farmhouse with its long white shed, the clump of purple phlox, and the white-flowered hop bush. At Old Point the road passed above the pines, and riders looked out on the site of what was once a major Indian village and a Jesuit outpost of New France.

Conductor Dexter Foster always took time to point out the monument to Father Rales, rising where once a palisaded Abenaki village had stood. Dexter liked nothing better than to collect a group of children and describe how the Indian women had planted their corn and the men had heated pitch to mend the birch-bark canoes, or how the chapel bell from the stockaded village called them to mass and councils of war. Noses would be pressed against the glass before he finished.

Dex Foster was one of the Somerset's first conductors. As a young man he had panned gold near Sacramento, but he found the livery business more profitable. After several of his stables burned, Dexter turned to driving a stage for Wells Fargo. Coming back to Maine, he settled in Anson. Every young woman who rode to work at the Madison mills on Dexter's train went through the same initiation. He would look at her ticket, shake his head, and declare that he was terribly sorry, but her ticket was no good; he would have to stop the train and put her off. Young ladies got very flustered on their first trip to Madison. One woman remembered Dexter for the good-natured joshing she got every morning. She had a pair of high-heeled white boots that she never had time to lace until she was aboard the train. Dexter liked to come along and lend fatherly advice.

From its founding, Madison was a river town born in the roar of the falls, with its 11,500 horsepower of nearly unharnessed energy pouring past until a dam was built. In freshets there was too much Kennebec. In 1897 a flood carried away thirty million feet of logs and every boom in the river, and the Somerset lost a great deal of trackage between Solon and Bingham. But it was the river that had provided transportation before the railroad arrived, and the river gave power to the industry that was to transform Madison.

In 1920 Holman Day was in Madison where scenes from his *Rider of the King Log* were being filmed. It was an authentic place for a logging romance, or at least it had been. By this date the real logging had moved north, and pulp was feeding the Madison paper mills–thousands of cords of four-foot wood brought south by the railroad. But when the Somerset first arrived, logging was still king in Madison and Weston was the big name. B. P. J. Weston and his brothers, to be precise. The name was painted in big black letters below the third-story windows of the hotel that sat up the hill from the tracks. Lumbermen, rivermen, salesmen, and sportsmen signed the register at the Weston House. In the adjacent barn ten pairs of oxen might be chewing their cuds and awaiting their toil in the woods to the north. From the Weston House you could look upriver and see, in the great curving sweep of the Kennebec, the line of stone cribs that secured the log booms. The smooth current flowed around them, one behind the other like an anchored flotilla of gunboats. Westward and down the hill was Madison's growing economy. First came the woolen mills, then the sulfite pulp mill, and finally, at the end of the century, the paper mills.

Madison had not raised any money for the Somerset. In all fairness, as the railroad spiked its rails toward the village, the town of Madison was in no condition to be generous. Over twelve thousand dollars in public funds had been "misplaced." Be that as it may, it was Anson across the river that had invested so much in the railroad. (The *Bangor Whig and Courier* reported the figure as eighty thousand dollars.) Its citizens were assured the line would not pass through Madison but cross the Kennebec at Fisher Falls below the village. The construction gangs began to build the approach to this bridge, and all seemed to be well for Anson. Then the railroad's management announced that the Fisher Falls crossing was not practical; the rails would have to pass through Madison before crossing to Anson. A yell went up from the Anson side of the river– but it was apparently drowned out by the roar of the falling river, which had favored Madison with the best power sites. The folks in Anson were assured that Madison would not have a station unless the citizens chose to construct one themselves. After eight town meetings, Madison voted not to build a depot.

For six years the Somerset kept its word. Trains slowed down at the main street crossing, and the mail was thrown off and swung on. Just across the river Anson's station, which was appropriately named Riverview, became a center of action. That action, however, was shared with the new railhead in the village of North Anson. (Anson and North Anson were the same municipality.) There J. C. Fuller's store became the fashion center for the upper Kennebec with ready-made garments from New York–long wool skirts trimmed with velvet and tight-fitting jackets with long rows of buttons from high neck to waist.

With the growing industry, Madison got its station. It wasn't very grand. One Tim Otis knocked it off its posts when–not realizing the switch had been thrown–he backed a train down the dead-end spur. Later a violent July storm of wind and hail blew the station down. If the whirlwind storm was an act of the little gods who favored Anson, then they acted after the fact. By 1892 a special train had been put on to clear the Madison Yard. Four years later the Somerset had its first regular train running at night as far as Madison. Then, in 1900, Madison got a new station, the only brick depot on the line. That same year one of the town's churches, rather naively, showed the first moving picture ever seen in the area. Electric lights for the whole town were just two years away.

After the Carrabassett tumbles over upturned ledge, the river meets the Kennebec at North Anson. Ben Foster painted a picture of the Carrabassett cascading beside an elm-shaded street of his hometown and passing beneath the covered bridge that carried the Somerset across the water. Foster called his painting *Lulled by the Murmuring Stream*. It is tempting to think that the title applied to the Somerset, which was to take twelve years getting across the river, but in economic truth the railroad was exhausted.

The new railhead had all the necessary facilities: a combination passenger-freight station, a carhouse, engine house, turntable, water tank, and long woodshed for storing the two-foot sticks used to fuel the locomotives. From the depot, stages left for Solon, Bingham, and Moosehead Lake. Westering toward the blue cones of Bigelow Mountain was William Atkinson's route to Canada through New Portland, Stratton, and a place called Jerusalem (which has since become the Carrabassett Valley ski area). Neither broad- nor narrow-gauge rails ever ran west from North Anson, but the traffic by stage and buckboard was considerable. Later, when automobiles came along, Al Wing's car (affectionately called "Jenney") made regular trips from North Anson to Flagstaff.

A trip up or down the dirt road beside the Carrabassett in summer was pleasant, but in winter it was a numbing experience. On a winter morning when the snow crunched, Agent Eames would arrive at his station as the first light of morning was turning the east white and clear as a mountain spring. His first concern was the ram-down stove that, when red hot, could make itself felt in the small waiting room. When the stage from North New Portland arrived with the horses blowing clouds of vapor, there was a rush for the stove as if it were the last heat in Maine. One lady got a bit too close. Much to her horror, the front of her dress began to char. Fortunately, Eames was safe behind the ticket window's bars.

The "new" North Anson station, built after the Somerset had crossed the
Carrabassett River in its push northward. Al Wing's "Jenney" is parked
on the far left, ready to take passengers to Flagstaff.
AUTHOR'S COLLECTION

"Madam," Eames said when he got the chance, "I calculate to keep this
waiting room so hot that it will make anybody sweat just to look in the window."
The woman was not impressed.

Hotel, grain depot, busy freight shed, North Anson gradually became a
thriving village. In 1882 the Somerset delivered a boiler for the new shank mill.
Steam from this boiler would also run the pump that forced water both into
hydrants along the main street and into a carriage wash operated for a nickel in
the slot. Farmers began to think about the benefits of regular hours, and their
wives of village advantages for their daughters.

Stations became places to congregate, to hear the news, to surreptitiously
turn over a freight tag and discover who had been so extravagant as to buy
rubber-tired buggy wheels, and to be present when, with whistle and bell, that
steam-throbbing connection with the rest of the world came and went.

Lester Bosworth, down from his farm above Fahi Pond, sat one morning
in the waiting room of Embden Station passing the time of day. Talk turned to

fighting, and one of the fellows claimed he could lick Lester. He kept pestering until he got on Lester's nerves. Lester upended the fellow over the stove. "Lester," said the fighter when he had picked himself up, "we'd better stop this. Someone's going to get hurt."

Life was congenial down at the depot; only occasionally did bad things happen. They used to point to a stain on the outside corner of the Embden depot where the station agent was murdered, but that's a story for another chapter.

You had to be very fortunate to be at the station when there was a real scoop to be had. Amos Campbell, the stage driver from Bingham to Skowhegan, arrived at Bingham Station one morning. The agent glanced up from the ticket window when Amos came in and asked him, as a joke, if he were taking the train. The agent was surprised when Amos said that he was. His sister, he explained, had come down with a bad sickness.

"Didn't know you had a sister," responded the agent.

"Oh, yes, lives in Waterville. She's the one we don't talk much about, but kin is kin when they are deathly ill." Amos bought a one-way ticket. As he went out, he spoke pleasantly to one of the conductors' wives who was sitting on the settee with her husband's lunch pail and a change of uniform in her lap; and all the while he had that wad of express money in his hip pocket–six hundred dollars! It left with him on the morning train. Later it was said that he had gone west.

That was news, but the Nortage murder was real tragedy. It got talked about until the story was worn out by years of telling. As brakeman Adrian Robinson told reporters when they came up on the train, you could see that there was trouble coming by the very look in Nortage's dark and evil eyes. Adrian told the reporters a lot of stuff like that, and they took it all down. Nortage came into Bingham on the morning train and made straight for the hotel where his wife was working. He found her sweeping in the lobby and took her by the shoulders. When she refused to come with him, he shot her five times.

The sheriff figured that Nortage would cross the Kennebec on the railroad bridge at Solon, and sent a telegram asking that a watch be posted. But Nortage fooled those waiting for him by crossing the river on the logs. The sheriff's posse finally cornered him in a barn over in North New Portland, where he used his sixth bullet on himself.

By 1886 communications had taken wings in the upper Kennebec Valley. Messages flowed on the wires beside the track. Station agents became telegraphers, often remarkably proficient and often busy at the key. It could be exciting stuff. Cryptic messages to and from the management of the paper mill at

Solon to a certain Friglar in London, England, for example, gave the station master his chance to use the transatlantic cablegrams with the two-inch seal of the Postal Telegraph-Cable Company emblazoned on the top of the forms.

Uncoded but more urgent was a summons for Dr. Paul from the Paterson family. Not to be forgotten was a message from Mrs. Mill: Her husband was to meet her on the night train. Vittum & Sons had word of "extra nice white halibut" from the American Halibut Company in Gloucester, and Joel Pierce was told with remarkably few words that his mother was dead. Mr. Day, at the paper mill, wired his partner that the wheels were turning once more at the mill and he was going upriver to do some fishing.

So the messages came and went. The swallows rested like iridescent clothespins on the wires beside the tracks, and life in the valley went on, soon taking new marvels for granted and returning attention to its own exigencies and concerns.

But changes were quietly and inexorably taking place, and the Somerset was a major vehicle in bringing them. The first train out of Bingham—on July 13, 1890—consisted of ten cars of last blocks (used in the making of shoes). Though the village still looked the same, there was increased traffic upon its elm-arched streets as well as a new pulse of expectation. The time would come when Sprague Mace, tacking a rough course up Bingham's main street, tipped his hat to a mannequin in a store window—a blatant liberty for which, in a more sober moment, he apologized.

With the coming of the trains, the hotel proprietor saw the need for a conveyance between the depot and his accommodations. The hotel hack was a wagon with the sides boarded up and roofed over. It was nothing to show off, which was maybe why it was painted a rusty red. It was an irksome fact to the people of Bingham that Solon had a bright red hotel carriage with upholstered seats. Still, if you were going on a trip of consequence and wanted to be anyone at all in the village, you had the hack call around. A roll of canvas could be let down over the open rear, but it shut out the air and was seldom used, even when it poured. Inside the hack two planks ran lengthwise so that passengers sat facing each other and toe-to-toe. The visiting dentist, laboring to board the hack with his collapsible drill always got tripped at least twice before he found a seat.

The hack's big evening came on Monday, which was drummers' night in Bingham. The salesmen descended upon the village, and their trunks—filled with a range of goods from foundation garments to pocketknives—demanded an extra wagon. With the drummers packed into the hotel hack like the goods in their traveling trunks, the procession up Bingham's main street began. The mail wagon brought up the rear with the express messenger sitting on the back, his

**Bingham Yard was the Somerset's railhead for fourteen years.
In the background, the freight station is on the right, while the
passenger station is on the left.** AUTHOR'S COLLECTION

feet dangling over the open tailgate and his tin box held tightly in his lap. He
marked their progress with long brown darts of tobacco juice–far more of a
deterrent to anyone who might have designs on the box than the revolver that
the messenger had strapped across his suspenders.

The 6:05 passenger train is in, the switching has been done, backs have
bent over the turntable's push bars, and the engine is backed into its house. The
sun is getting low over Fletcher Mountain, and the cinders underfoot are beginning to cool after the heat of the day. There the smell of sun-warmed creosote
and a whiff of coal smoke mixes with something good being fried in the buggy
(caboose). With a rounding clang, a horseshoe circles the iron stake and settles
down to cover Magoon's ringer. Tupper hasn't lost his touch after all.

Chapter Four

LIFE IN THEM GOOD OLD DAYS

THEY SAT IN A RING of lantern light–a small circle surrounded by the darkness of the engine house. Talk turned to the latest news.

The Skowhegan Ghost had been caught after haunting the countryside for nearly a month. It had been seen crossing the road and glimpsed in the shadows of many farmyards. Once or twice it had pressed its white face to a windowpane, only to vanish at the cry of alarm. The spook had been proven to be human in most respects–crazy but harmless, a thin, lost shadow of a man who claimed to be already dead, having been killed at Cold Harbor, or perhaps it was Shiloh. His only possessions were two muskets, both without locks, and a small tin dark-lantern (the flashlight of the wick-and-oil days) that he would not let out of his grasp. The whole time the sheriff plied him with questions, he kept opening the lantern's shutter as if to reassure himself that the flame still burned.

The engine-house conversation shifted westward to Smithfield, where a man had just died of the "dry mortifications." It was a strange affliction that started at his toes and crept slowly up to his neck before killing him. "Damned thorough," was the engine wiper's comment.

It was late, almost nine-thirty, when Al Skillings told a fish story. That very summer, it seems, he had caught a whopper of a trout on a piece of his own red flannels. Al wore his long johns all year, so there was no reason to doubt the story. Someone did say that there are dumb members of every species, even trout.

Cap Crowell turned the face of his pocket watch to the lantern light. It was past time to turn in. The group left the engine wiper to bank his fires and brew tea over a shovel of coals. The wind went on making ghosts around the smoke jacks. As for the morrow, its events were preordained.

Most of the Somerset men with whom I have talked were fatalists who knew how to laugh. If the former was a defense against uncertainty, then the latter was certainly a necessity. Fatalism made sense. Often you could look back and see how events had woven together into a preordained plot, and before you knew what was taking place you were having one of those days "when it don't pay to get up." Sometimes a person got killed or died and didn't have time to think at all.

It was one of those days of fateful events when Arthur Tupper got fired. It all began months before, when Duffer Merrill took over as conductor on Arthur's train. It soon became apparent that Duffer had passed his prime. Time and again he gave the high ball against the orders he had tucked away and for-

Arthur Tupper and his crew, photographed April 21, 1910, at Kineo Station. The engine is No. 12, and she is pulling passenger train No. 16. From left to right are fireman Ed Magoon; engineer Arthur Tupper; an unnamed baggage clerk; brakeman Adrian Robinson; and conductor "Duffer" Merrill. All were later fired for running a meet above Austin Junction. AUTHOR'S COLLECTION

gotten in his pocket. Among the crew only Arthur seemed to worry about this. As rear-end brakeman Adrian Robinson remembered, everyone figured that Arthur'd never forget.

It was forest-fire season, and the railroad was using oil-burning engines above Bingham. The practice was for trains to swap a coal burner for an oil-fired locomotive at Austin Junction just below Bingham. While the engines were being changed, the conductor should have gone into a little building that looked much like an outhouse and checked the register book. Trains coming south off the mountain registered before backing into Bingham Yard. Trains heading north up the grade to Deadwater were also required to "book." This way, you could tell if the main line above Bingham was clear.

When they reached the Junction that morning, Arthur and his fireman transferred their lunch pails and tool box to the waiting oil burner and coupled to the train. With them was P. G. Smith, the master mechanic, making his annual inspection and riding in the cab. Smith was especially interested in the oil-burner mechanisms, as they had been giving trouble. Arthur had his hands full. They had orders to wait at the Junction for the down train to clear the line. It hadn't, a fact that Duffer would've known if he'd remembered to check the register book. No one thought to check on the conductor—including, for the first time, Arthur Tupper.

As they started up the grade to Bingham Heights, Adrian Robinson thought momentarily about the orders, but he was preoccupied—good-looking Effie Jane had promised to be at the Heights and to wave.

They hadn't gone many train lengths before Arthur saw the smoke of the down train. He shoved in the throttle, flipped the air-brake handle clear over, and pulled on the whistle cord. The trains stopped with no more between them than room to walk between the opposing engines.

Arthur turned to Smith. "I'd like to turn in my resignation," he said.

"I'll accept it," the master mechanic replied.

But the Somerset was no longer its own road, and the Portland office of the Maine Central wasn't satisfied. The whole crew, one for all and all for one, got the ax.

So there you are. Arthur Tupper's last day as a railroad engineer had come. He finished the run to Kineo Station. "I suppose it was childish," Arthur told me, "but I knew it was my last chance, and I blew the whistle at the smallest excuse all the way to Rockwood."

There were plenty of similar opportunities to nurture fatalistic beliefs. Railroading is a dangerous occupation. Even in the later years the number of men killed and injured on the Somerset is appalling. Between 1908 and 1910, for instance, five men were killed and thirteen injured. One cause of accidents was the daily practice of dangerous tricks that tempted fate. The use of push poles was high on the list of these questionable practices. These poles were carried on the sides of the locomotive tenders and were used when you wanted to move cars on an adjacent track. A push pole was angled from a shallow socket on the buffer beam at the front of the engine to the car on the next track. If the pole slipped or broke and a man was standing anywhere nearby, disaster could happen fast.

In the good old days before automatic couplers, "pulling the pin" was a very manual operation with an appetite for fingers. The mechanism was simple. The link was an iron bar with one end attached to the car, not unlike a long, narrow hinge. The free end of this link had a hole; once the link rested in the socket of the car being attached, a pin was dropped through this hole. It was the last-second guiding of the link into the socket that put fingers in jeopardy, but the real danger lay in having to stand between the cars when coupling. Link-and-pin couplers were used on the Somerset's service cars until 1907; they were standard equipment on the dangerous log bunks throughout the history of the railway. More will be said about these notorious log bunks in a later chapter.

Photos show the "catwalks" along the tops of the old railroad cars, and all of us have seen in a western some dramatic and desperate flight or fight upon the rooftop of a swaying railroad coach. Before air brakes, "walking the cars" was part of a trainman's working day. One blast of the whistle meant "down brakes," and the brakeman ran along the traintop, setting the brakes on each car. Darkness added peril, and freezing sleet could make the task next to suicidal. Ashes were strewn over the narrow walks when ice was accumulating, but even then it took courage to walk the cars. To warn brakemen on car roofs that the train was about to pass through a covered bridge, the Somerset hung telltales–a sort of coarse-toothed comb of wires–over the tracks. Those wires felt like Medusa's hair across your face on a bitter cold night, but of course this was better than being slammed into a bridge.

"Switching on the fly" was a neat trick with potential for trouble. It was a common practice on the Somerset because of the railroad's many dead-end spurs. The train moved forward and at the correct instant, the brakeman "pulled the pin" on the cars to be set off. The engine then accelerated to clear the switch to the spur with the remainder of the train. Once the switch was cleared, it was thrown to allow the detached cars to roll onto the spur. Crews prided themselves in their ability to perform the maneuver with as little time lost as possible.

**The north portal of the covered bridge spanning the Carrabassett River
at North Anson. That's the "new" passenger station on the right.**
AUTHOR'S COLLECTION

There was another time-saving method of setting off cars on a siding running in the direction opposite to that of the working train. It was being used the day that Lorney Sawtell was killed on the spur to Dodling Quarry. The tactic was to back the car or cars onto the spur; at the moment when the engineman set the straight air brake on the locomotive, the brakeman would pull the pin to let the desired cars roll on down the siding. It was one of those split-second maneuvers. When the brake was set on the locomotive, a slowing action traveled from car to car, and for a moment the linkage changed from pushing the next car to being slack. This was the instant to pull the pin.

No one knew exactly what happened that day. Lorney had mentioned not feeling very well when he came to work that morning–perhaps that was it, or perhaps the brake took more suddenly than he expected. Or perhaps, as many said, his day had come. At any rate, Lorney was kneeling over the end of a flatcar where the pin was to be pulled. He toppled over and fell under the train.

51

The engineman on that train spoke during his failing years of the "man I killed." Of course he hadn't, but it bothered him all the same, and again he would feel as he felt that morning on the spur to Dodling Quarry.

The year 1908 was the Somerset's most tragic. It began on May 28 when Lester Goodridge, a young fireman, was killed at Oakland. Lester left an invalid mother to look after herself as best she might.

The following month death came to Deadwater. Willy Wood was a promising young railroader–very young to be the conductor of a log train. His father, Robert, was a section foreman, and his grandfather had been an Irish immigrant. Willy's mother had met Robert at a North Anson boarding house where she was a chambermaid. She was young enough to be his daughter, but both families were pleased. When Willy was a small boy, his folks gave him a little book that spoke in fine print of sin and faith and hell. Boys were expected to grow up fast in those days. That morning at Deadwater, Conductor Wood signaled the engine forward, stepped back, and caught his heel in a switch frog. He was an only child.

On July 16 Ed Magoon did not miss his redheaded fireman right away. Jack McSorley had gone back to check the water in the tank. It was hot, and Ed figured his fireman had gone on to the baggage car, where there was always a large bottle of Poland Spring water. (This fringe benefit was furnished by the Ricker brothers, who owned the springs and had a large interest in the railroad.) But when the train pulled into Moxie and the fireman had not returned to ring the bell, Ed felt there was something wrong. Confirmation came when they stopped at the station and McSorley could not be found. They put cars on the turnout and ran the engine back over the twisting curves below the station. One of the passengers made remarks about the delay–something about a "hick railroad"–but when the engine returned and the crew was laying McSorley's body on the baggage wagon, that same passenger came over and helped.

Skip Houdlet was the fireman on the return run, and the engineer and the locomotive were the same. Houdlet stepped back, lost his footing, and fell out the gangway. He managed to grab the handrail and swung several times before his feet found the steps. Engine number 12 with its wickedly short decking had almost caused its second fatal accident in one day.

Three young men in as many months and then, in August, another. Lee Baker, baggage master, was killed while helping to couple the cars at Kineo. Lee's father, old "Maj" Baker, had come through the Civil War unscathed because (according to him) he was so short that the enemy fired over his head. Now his son had been killed. Four men, none over twenty-five, had been lost in one year.

Early on the Somerset began to improve its equipment. By 1898, for instance, Miller and Trojan couplings (which joined automatically) replaced the old links and pins on most of the rolling stock. The following year Westinghouse air brakes were installed on passenger cars, and a start was made at placing these brakes on the freight equipment. But the men knew that fate still worked in the misplaced step.

Brakeman Adrian Robinson was doing some switching on a black night at Bingham. It happened as suddenly as a knife slips. Adrian had just waved the engine ahead and was swinging onto the pilot step when he thought he saw the engineer motion to him. In the second he looked up at the cab, his foot missed the step and his leg went under the pilot. The engine was in motion by this time. Adrian grabbed the pilot's bars and kept himself from being pulled under the front of the locomotive. In the beam of the headlamp, he saw the silver curve of the next guide rail to a switch. He knew without thinking what this meant. When they came to the guide, he would be drawn under the black bulk of the engine and its grinding wheels. He could do nothing but hang on and yell. It was his shouting that saved him. Ralph O'Hara heard and waved his lantern wildly, and the engineer slammed the air-brake lever into the emergency notch. Adrian had a black-and-blue leg, but he was alive.

In a more playful mood, fate seems to have enjoyed experimenting with the cow scenario. One passenger had just made his own dent in the frayed plush seat of a Somerset coach when the train came to a stop. After what seemed like a long delay, the conductor returned to the coach, a little out of breath, to report that a cow had been on the tracks. The train started up, only to stop again.

"Another cow?" the passenger asked when the conductor returned for the second time.

"Nope," answered the conductor, "same one."

Mixed train number 4 lumbered up the grade from Bombazee Rips to Norridgewock. Suddenly the engineman thrust in the throttle. The fireman swung the fire door shut and leaned out the gangway, expecting to see the headlamp of another engine heading toward them for a "cornfield meet." Instead he saw a small girl and a cow. The girl had a firm grip on the animal's tail and appeared to be steering it for home. To the fireman's admiration, the engineman curbed his language. The girl never looked back; she had been sent to bring in that straying cow, and the shortest route was down the Somerset's track. In procession they went until girl and cow reached the lane to the farm.

Incidentally this same girl, who grew up to become Mrs. Haskell, also fell through the stringers of the Norridgewock railroad bridge not long afterward.

Brought home, she lay unconscious for days and then awoke to announce she would like some bread and butter. In 1962 Mrs. Haskell was ninety-one years old.

Obviously the Somerset was not the only railroad that had problems with cows. All railways were obligated to maintain fences when they passed through farms. Occasionally cow underpasses were built, including a rather grand two-portaled granite affair just below Bingham Heights Station. Sometimes the Somerset negotiated a deal with the farmer—a onetime fifty-dollar payment that would exempt the railroad from any further liability.

Locomotives were all equipped with "cowcatchers"—plow-shaped prows of wood and iron bolted to the front of the engines. Later these cowcatchers were reduced to "pilots" and lost their elegance. There was more to a cowcatcher than just looks. *The Science of Railways* (1904 edition) noted that "while this device often fails to accomplish the purpose for which it is designed, it is in the main beneficial." The purpose was to clear obstructions, including cows, from the rails and so ward off derailments.

It took skill to hit a cow correctly with a light engine—not that any engine-man coveted a row of notches carved in his throttle handle. Still, brakes were poor, fences inadequate, and cows numerous. An engineman was bound to hit a cow sooner or later. According to those with experience, if you couldn't stop,

Engine No. 3, the *Norridgewock*, lies beside the tracks in a ditch after hitting a cow at milepost 19. AUTHOR'S COLLECTION

then you should hit hard enough to bounce the animal off the cowcatcher. Striking slowly seldom saved the cow. Instead its carcass was apt to roll under the pilot truck and upset the engine.

Arthur Tupper knew this. His train was rolling down the grade from Embden to Caratunk Falls. The fireman was busy using this chance to fill the oil cups and blow lubricant into the cylinders. By the time Arthur saw the cow from his side, he knew he couldn't stop. He blew the whistle as a gesture of goodwill, opened the throttle, and said a little prayer. The cow went end-over-end into Alder Brook; the engine took the jar and sped on.

Ed Millar, on his first passenger run, was not so lucky. He tried to stop. They had run into a summer cloudburst just north of Anson Station and Ed was taking it slowly—sticking his head out the cab window was like thrusting it into a waterfall. They were almost on the cow before Ed saw it. Still, he thought he might be able to stop. A very short time later the locomotive was over on her side, half buried in the soft fill. Ed and his fireman crawled out from the cab while the conductor ran back to the station to summon help. Actually the situation could have been a great deal worse. The coaches were still on the iron, and the thrown engine was well out of the way. The passengers were taken to the next station to wait while the track was inspected and a locomotive sent out to finish the run.

Old Cap Crowell, when he wasn't so old, was the best engineman the Somerset had, but a cow managed to dump him. This time it was a real mess, though no one got seriously hurt. The railroad hired a team of horses to help get the locomotive, old *Bombazeen,* back on the rails. The track was closed for two days.

Occasionally the trains had affairs with buggies, wagons, and, with increasing frequency, cars. As the engines grew larger, the odds turned more and more in their favor. The Somerset was obliged to hold hearings and get permission to cross public roads at grade level. Apparently it wasn't difficult to obtain permission—even when, as in one case, the railroad admitted that it had forgotten to ask until the roadbed was completed. There were only two crossings with watchmen, one in Norridgewock and the other in Madison. The latter was established shortly after J. K. Mckenner and his team of horses had a narrow miss.

Just above Austin Junction, the Somerset crossed the dirt road leading to the Goodrich Farm and a number of other homesteads scattered between the folding hills east of Bingham. It was in many ways typical of the many one-lane dirt roads the track crossed, and had the usual sign announcing that the public passed at its own risk. However, the risk at Goodrich Crossing was increased by the sidehill approach. A few weeks after a buggy had been demolished and a horse killed there, Engineman John Vigue forgot to blow the whistle as he approached the crossing. He was promptly called on the carpet (which is just a saying, as the Somerset president's office did not have a carpet). John got a week's rest without pay for the oversight. This wasn't much, but it would sharpen the boys up.

The next accident involved a car. As was often the case, the cause was driver error. People learned to drive by trial, error, and sometimes a lesson from the car salesman—once around the barnyard and through the pasture fence. At Goodrich Crossing a new driver hit the wrong pedal and landed in front of the westbound freight. The locomotive pushed the crumpled automobile down over the bank. A runner was sent to fetch help.

"How's the driver?" Agent Pearl Woodard asked when the messenger reached the station.

"We hain't got him out yet, but I suspect he's dead," the runner panted.

They got the car turned over on one side and the door pried open.

"Are you hurt, Carl?" Pearl asked when they lifted the driver out and could see who he was.

"Why, damn, Pearl, can't you see I'm about half kilt?"

After a while Carl walked back to the station with the agent to give the particulars for the report.

There were some who never did get into the habit of stopping at railroad crossings. Hermie Baker was bringing a sled load of firewood down the road that crossed the track just above the depot at Bingham Heights. His helper, Alty Robinson, was riding on the rear sled runner. It was cold as all get-out; both men had the flaps of their caps pulled tightly over their ears and were looking straight ahead, intent on the hot beans waiting at home. The team and its load landed on the rails in conjunction with a down train easing into the Heights. Stovewood flew in all directions, and Alty landed under a boxcar sitting on the siding. The only injury was his dislocated shoulder.

"Godfry-mighty, Alty," Hermie burst out as he bent over to help his friend out from under the boxcar, "what a place to meet a train."

When it came to hitting things, Somerset engines had a proclivity for smashing cabooses. At one time the Somerset was down to two.

There were cars to pick up one evening at the Madison mill. The caboose, several flatcars, and the Somerset's homemade donkey crane, or boomcar, were set off while the task was being done. Reed Hilton and the conductor were in the caboose getting supper. Both supposed they'd been left on a turnout. If they realized they'd been left sitting on the main line, of course, they would have been out flagging as both common sense and the rules dictated. When the North

Anson Extra came across the bridge running ten miles an hour faster than the yard limit allowed, it slammed into the flatcars, which in turn sent the donkey crane splintering through the caboose with its upright boiler splitting the roof in two. Reed took a header out one of the side doors, and the conductor a flying leap out the other. That was one advantage with the old four-door cabooses: There was a better chance for bailing out.

When Foreman Spurgeon Hoar arrived from Oakland with the wreck crew, he pushed his derby hat forward and gave the back of his head a thorough scratching. "Now that's what I call a hell of a mess" was his appraisal. Reed Hilton, who had landed facedown in a mudhole green with the contribution of horses, agreed. Actually, all considering, things worked out pretty well. The shattered caboose was already loaded on the crane ready for its last run to the junk pile.

It is an open question who ran the greater risk, the train crew involved in an accident or the crew that was hustled together and sent out to put things right. The Somerset had no heavy cranes for dealing with wrecks. By and large the work was done with bull chains, rerailers, jacks, cables, pulleys, blocking, temporary track, and ingenuity. In winter a man put on everything he had and waded through the snow, hauling cables and lugging timbers. In summer he stripped to his undershirt and squinted through his own sweat. Whatever the conditions, danger awaited in every pile of blocking and each stretched cable.

Yet contrivance by contrivance, many of the crude working conditions on the Somerset became history. It was, after all, the era of inventions and progress. Not all the intended improvements worked, of course. For example, there was the clothes-washing apparatus that an inventive trainman set up in the Bingham engine house. Washing frocks and overalls was a real chore for men away from home as well as for those who had no wives or willing lady friends. This particular trainman got hold of a steel barrel and connected a pipe that could be fed with steam from a locomotive. With great agitation, suds, and clouds of steam, the apparatus took on its first load of clothes. It cleaned them perfectly and filled them with small holes like a sieve.

Among the instruments that really worked–and perhaps transformed life up and down the valley as much as any other invention, either now or then–was the telephone. A phone line was strung on Somerset poles from Norridgewock to Madison in 1887 and to North Anson by 1897. While the railway stuck to its telegraph for official communication, and while some people got surprised when their messages were heard by others, the phone was more than handy.

One westbound freight pulled out of Bingham Yard against orders to wait for an eastbound train. The station agent got to a phone and cranked hard for the

**As they work on an overturned car just north of Bingham Heights, a
Maine Central Railroad wreck crew takes time out for a picture.**
AUTHOR'S COLLECTION

central operator. He knew that the Hugheses on their trackside farm below town
had just put in a phone. Walter Hughes was an exceptionally long-legged youth,
and he made use of this advantage in getting down to the track. The freight had
just come into view, and Walter flagged it with a red bandanna.

But the more modern the Somerset became, the less colorful (literally) it
was. When the railroad reached Bingham in 1890, it was still in the "signal-
book" era. Signal books were kept at Oakland, North Anson, and Bingham, and
all conductors entered their trains, the times they booked in, and the colors of
any signals that their trains might bear. The system was crucial in that it let the
following trains know who was on the line and approximately where they were.
There was room in these books to scrawl a comment or two. One conductor
wrote: "Tim ran out of tobacco this trip." That would be Tim Otis, well known
for his chewing habit. The next conductor, who evidently had walked the cars
behind Tim, added, "Remember to thank the Lord for small favors!"

Station agents, section crews, and train crews making a meet kept watch for
the signal flags flapping on the pilot beams of engines as they passed. Even in old
age, when much of the past and the present had become confused in his mind, one

Somerset man could repeat the flag code: "Wild trains will wear a blue flag, trains with sections following will wear red, and trains running against each other will wear white." *Wild train* is an old term for what was later called an extra train. Perhaps the original name was dropped because of its unfortunate connotations.

Before the advent of order boards with their semaphore arms raised over the depot roofs, a station agent hung out a red flag or a lantern with a red globe when he wanted to stop a train. For ten minutes after a train's passing, the agent was required to show a blue flag or lantern.

The old Somerset regulations had thirty-three rules, including one in bold print, that dealt with the responsibility of returning switches to their normal, mainline positions. Many of these rules, such as the requirement that all conductors be at the saloon brake whenever a train approached a station or a flag stop, were obsolete by the time the Maine Central took over in 1911. Not to worry: The new management brought with it a very thick book of regulations, some of which also sounded out of date. There was a rule against gambling on passenger trains and against card playing of any kind on Sunday; another warned enginemen against allowing any unnecessary noises or escapes of steam that might scare horses. Many Somerset men found the new rules hard to memorize, and some found them difficult to read. A few trainmen's wives made some spending money helping these fellows prepare for examinations.

By 1911 the signal days were past. Signal books were replaced by forms with just space enough for the required information, and the signal flags were used as grease rags at the Oakland shops.

I had a friend, an old railroader, who often spoke of "them good old days on the Somerset," but how good were they? Certainly there was little safe or soft in them. Most railroad men tended to be lean. Pat Hursey was a very large exception. Finding the facilities at Deadwater Station occupied, Pat squeezed into a coach toilet and had to be chopped out with a fire ax. But Pat was an engineman for whom making new holes in one's belt was an occupational hazard.

In general, the less glamorous the job, the harder you worked physically. The fireman on the North Anson Extra, for instance, shoveled six tons of coal from tender to firebox on each daily round from Oakland to Bingham. Or consider the unsung labors of the section crews. Each morning and all along the line backs bent to pump the three-wheeled velocipedes. The rails had to be inspected regardless of the cold or rain. The velocipedes did have an advantage. They were light. If you suddenly met an extra train, one hard lean would flip you and your vehicle safely off the track—a double advantage because the railroad held the sectionman responsible for equipment.

And that was just the start of the day. "Tonging in" new rail by hand (installing it by means of tongs, which allowed two men—one on each side of a rail that weighed perhaps six hundred pounds—to lift together), replacing ties, tamping ballast, tearing out beaver dams that were plugging culverts, or stirring up mile upon mile of blackflies with a bush scythe sent many young men to find other work. Those who stayed, settled into a seasonal routine as regular as the section foreman who always ate lunch from his dinner bucket top downward, beginning with the pie.

Still, a feeling deeper than nostalgia is evoked when looking backward to the good old days along the Somerset. It has to do with the people—their resourcefulness, their responsibility, their often rough but fundamental goodness, and their ability to laugh.

And finally, there is the romance that lingers in the memories of this past. . . . The moths flutter around the oil lamps along the station platform. You seem to hear—and then are certain of—the rumble of the train easing down the grade from Deadwater. Rising and falling, wrapped in the warm summer night, there come the sounds of the whistle at Mayfield Crossing. A few minutes more and there is light moving in the branches of the trees, and then suddenly the circle of a headlamp brighter than the full moon. The polished rails run silver.

The ties sink perceptibly under the weight of the locomotive. The engine passes, moving with the rhythm of its side rods and the ringing of its bell—a jarring mass, half alive and rolling from one human appointment to the next. The baggage master, sleeves rolled up and legs spread, is standing in the open door of his car. The lit windows of the coach slow to a halt. The light of the platform lamps is reflected in the gilt and varnish of the Pullman cars.

The conductor meets the station agent on the platform and now strides back along his train, a Knights Templar watch fob flashing reflections from the bulge of his broadcloth vest. He folds and folds again the tissue of a train order, then slips it between his finger and his wedding band. His lantern is up. The brakeman swings onto the coach platform with the step stool in one hand. There is the hiss of releasing air brakes.

A woman's face under an extraordinarily broad-brimmed hat encircled with ostrich feathers looks down from a passing window. In a sliding instant her eyes meet yours. And then the red glow of the tail lanterns disappears.

Chapter Five

⚮

RAILS ALONG THE AUSTIN

Birch Point at Rockwood is one of Maine's wonderful places. The wavelets wash in on the gravel of Barrows Bay; across the dancing surface of Moosehead Lake rises the majestic brow of Kineo. Here, on the first day of summer in 1906, a select group of men and their wives gathered to view the Somerset's new terminus. William Ayer, the railway superintendent, was one; the others were figures of power and influence—rich, well acquainted within the halls of legislature, and skilled in corporate manipulations.

There was Governor John Fremont Hill, who was born in Eliot, Maine, graduated from the Maine Medical School in 1878, interned at Long Island College Hospital in New York, and then practiced in Boothbay for a year. His father-in-law, Peleg Vickery, was a publisher; together Hill and Vickery founded a publishing firm that specialized in journals such as the *Fireside Visitor* and *Hearth and Home*. These magazines made money through skillful advertising, and they made a lot of it. Some felt that Hill's term as governor of Maine lacked luster, but his administration did manage to pay off the state's floating debt, incurred in the Spanish American War. He was, as one biographical sketch put it, "a business man with large and varied interests"—including railroads. In 1903 he became president of the Somerset.

Another member of the group was William T. Haines, who would also serve his state as governor. He was a graduate of the University of Maine (1876) and Albany Law School. He started practice in Oakland and rose steadily in both reputation and the importance of his clientele. He served as attorney general and a trustee of the University of Maine (supervising the building of Coburn and Wingate Halls), and was instrumental in founding a law school in Bangor. His reason for being at Rockwood that summer morning lay in his timberlands north of Bingham. He needed a means of transporting his logs.

61

Also present was J. C. Hutchinson. He was a smaller fish who represented the Coburn heirs—owners, among other things, of a fleet of steamboats on Moosehead and townships of prime forestland that would be serviced by the Somerset. Not surprisingly, knowing the Coburns, they owned the land at Rockwood upon which the Somerset was building its terminal.

In the second year of Hill's presidency the original Somerset Railroad had been sold to the holding company of which Haines was a principal director. This company had become the new Somerset Railway. With additional stock limits set, the railway was authorized to build through to Moosehead Lake as well as to operate steamboats, hotels, telegraph systems, and an express business. For these promoters it was a profitable deal. They would have a railway to bring their timber south, and one that the Maine Central Railroad would soon take off their hands. In 1907 the Maine Central endorsed a $1.5 million bond issue, thus buying control of the Somerset.

Not present in the party touring the new railhead, but certainly interested, were the Ricker brothers of Poland Spring Resort and springwater fame. Their water was sold in bottles molded into the form of a sage—who might well have been one of the bearded Rickers, whose timing and business sense had made their name synonymous with health and luxury. The brothers' opinions carried a good deal of weight with Maine Central management, and both the railroad and the Rickers had their eyes on the new Kineo House (hotel) just across the lake from Rockwood.

So the deal was all but done. The Somerset was about to double its trackage and assume the nickname of the "Kineo Short Line." Birch Point was an exciting place that June afternoon. Hutchinson was laying out streets, and there was already a village of tents housing construction crews. The railway was building a three-story hotel with a laundry in the basement, steam heat, gas lighting, and an icehouse. A three-story annex would feature a large dining room and forty iron beds to accommodate woodsmen at a dollar per night.

As for the railway itself, it had spanned the Kennebec for the fourth and last time. Track was being laid south from Rockwood to meet the rails coming north. The newspapers reported that "close to a thousand men were working on the construction." It was expected that the final spike would be driven before the snow fell—and indeed, the last spike was driven on November 15, 1906, at a point near Indian Pond. The first train entered Kineo Yard on December 3, and passenger service through to Kineo was authorized on February 2, 1907.

But building a railway up the Austin Valley and across the swamps north of

Deadwater had not been easy. The extension had cost well over a million and a half dollars and had taken its toll in human lives.

The Somerset had hired Henry Hill, a civil engineer and a graduate of M.I.T., to locate the new line to Moosehead Lake. Hill was noted for three things: long legs, drinking, and the ability to pick out the best of all possible railway routes. The engineering office was set up in a second-floor room overlooking Bingham's main street. These accommodations were across the street from the hotel—which was an advantage for those who had to board. There was a desk and a drafting table where Harry Beals, fresh out of college, worked on the mapping and computed the fills and cuts. In the meantime Hill was off to the north, blazing a path, collecting data, and leaving his survey crew panting behind. There was no keeping up with Henry Hill when he set out to locate a railroad.

Young John Ayer, whose father had been president of the Somerset, soon found out how tough it was to lay out a railroad through Maine's woods and swamps. His uncle, Bill Ayer, had offered him a summer job, and John reported to Henry Hill at Bingham early in June 1904. The survey party traveled over a corduroy tote road to Deadwater and took up quarters in an old logging camp. Their first morning started in the mist along the Austin somewhere close to six o'clock. John was put in charge of a crew and given the task of running levels to fix elevations along the proposed route. He didn't have much of a crew. The rodman was an old miner, and the two axmen were no younger. John quickly found that he couldn't keep up with the transit crew that was running the compass line. It was a hard first day, and at its close John checked his field notes and found that he had Austin Stream flowing uphill.

That evening Hill gave his new surveyor some needed schooling. The next day saw an improvement, but the country along the Austin was hard going. It consisted of what seemed to be a never-ending series of logans, bog holes, and stream banks tangled with alders. There were also thorn bushes as John discovered when his leap across a mud hole came up short. As days went on, one got used to the routine—washing clothes in a bucket, looking forward to beans and the cook's biscuits hot from the reflector oven, cutting boughs for a new bed, and sleeping to the whine of mosquitoes. By the end of summer, Hill's survey crew had laid out the railroad's path from Bingham to Moxie Pond.

John was back the following summer, working for Hill again. The survey party assembled in Greenville at the foot of Moosehead and sailed up the lake to the new base of operations at Birch Point in Rockwood. Their support crew consisted of a cook, a cookee, and axmen—all just off a log drive and decidedly the worse for wear. The survey party had to make do with the lunch they had brought until the cook was sober enough to prepare a meal.

At Birch Point they occupied an office camp abandoned by a lumber operation and went to bed early on bunks mattressed with fir boughs. During the night John was awakened when Hill began yelling that there was a bear on top of him. Hill often had nightmares, so John simply tried to calm him down by telling him—in the dark—that everything was all right. Hill kept hollering for someone to light a lantern and shoot the bear. When a member of the crew responded, the bear turned out to be a tremendous porcupine, an animal that was common in the area. John used to leave his transit on the job at night until a porcupine chewed off a tripod leg.

Needing to move their camp farther south, the crew loaded bateaux as heavily as they dared and headed down the West Branch of the Kennebec, subsequently disembarking near the point where the Somerset's track would cross the Canadian Pacific rails. John stepped in a hole while carrying a small barrel of flour around the dam at Long Pond and injured himself seriously enough to be laid up for several weeks. He ended the summer back at Bingham, running a transit for the construction crew.

From Bingham to Deadwater there was no choice as to route. The track would have to climb the twisting gorge of Austin Stream. During summer the Austin's volume dwindles and the sun bleaches its stony path. In a dry season you could call it a big brook, but in spring and during freshets the Austin becomes a river. For a few miles before joining the Kennebec, this stream meanders over the valley it has created; then the hills pinch in, and the Austin fills its steep-sided valley with the sound of its labors. The water churns from one pool to the next, and the whirlpools collect the foam into giant biscuits.

The principal problem for Hill and his crew was laying out a unified grade of $2\frac{1}{2}$ percent from Bingham to Deadwater—that is, a two-and-a-half-foot rise in elevation for each one hundred feet of trackage. A steeper though much shorter grade was necessary to get the tracks out of the Kennebec Valley and onto the first range of hills that edged Bingham to the east. The new trackage was to begin a mile below Bingham Yard at a spot that Will Ayer promptly named Austin Junction. From there the climb would start immediately. There would be a short reprieve at Bingham Heights, and then the rails would commence the eight-mile grade to Deadwater. Beyond this point the line followed a series of rises to the high point on the entire railroad, known as Bald Mountain Hill. Here the elevation is 1,125 feet, 773 feet above the valley floor at Bingham.

Curious locals pay a Sunday "visit" to the Italian camp in Moscow.
AUTHOR'S COLLECTION

With the beginning of construction in 1904, there rose a new settlement on the Hermie Baker's farm just above Bingham—a village of sod huts and tar-paper shanties built by the Italians working on the new right-of-way. It became the fashion for Bingham folks to hitch up the buggy or the two-seater on a Sunday afternoon and go take a look. These dark, short men gathered in small groups around their fires, did their own cooking, and played at their favorite game, pitching rocks at a target. They spoke little if any English.

The farmers close by were not amused. Smith's maple sap house had appeared in the Italians' camp, a board here and a board there. Nearby rail fences disappeared. Charges were brought and Dominic Susi, the boss, made his crew pay reparations. Deacon Elmer Baker took a different tack. He filled a couple of baskets with blowdown apples and passed the fruit out as the Italians were going to work. That evening they came by his farm and serenaded the deacon and his wife with harmonicas and an accordion.

Bread and beer were the supplied fare for these men. At the main camp on the Baker Farm, the bread was baked in a huge brick oven shaped like a beehive. The dough was mixed with a long-handled spade and molded into loaves on a board that also served as the cook's bunk. A fire was built inside the oven to heat its stone floor. Once this had been accomplished, the coals were raked out and the loaves laid on the stones. As construction moved on up the line, bread was still made in this oven and hauled north in a two-wheeled dumpcart.

It was common to see these men going to work still eating their breakfast with bottles of beer protruding from their hip pockets and long loaves of bread under their arms. Little wonder that small game disappeared wherever the Italians camped. They ate whatever they could run down, and occasionally their digestive tracts rebelled. The paymaster at the Deadwater camp checked on several men who were too sick for work. He found that they had boiled a hedgehog and a bittern (also known as a shitpoke in the vernacular) together. According to the sick men, it was the bittern that had laid them low. "Too much the big chick," they complained.

Dominic Susi literally swung a big stick. As long as he was around, all remained quiet. When one of his construction laborers went berserk in a camp store, just the sight of Dominic striding up the right-of-way was enough to sub-

An Italian construction crew digs down to ledge on the Somerset's new rail bed north of Bingham. RAYMOND L. FOLGER LIBRARY

due the fellow. One moment he was throwing chairs through the window, and the next he was jumping through the window himself and hiding in the woods. Dominic similarly quelled an uprising over wages that had broken out in the Deadwater camp, rounding up the two ringleaders and urging them along to the Bingham lockup with a pickax handle.

The boss who lost control was in trouble. Dominic found one crew sitting down on the job, their boss nowhere in sight. Hearing a pounding from a large wooden tool box, Dominic investigated and found the boss stuffed inside. The crew went back to work, but their boss disappeared. Dominic Susi did well for himself. A Bingham girl married him despite the fact that her family disowned her for it. He also built the Somerset's Bald Mountain spur, and later started a very successful construction business of his own.

The natives left the Italians (whom they called "Eye-talians") alone. The word was that these foreigners were a dangerous bunch who carried long knives in their boots. It was rumored that two of them lay buried in the big fill just south of Mayfield Crossing where they had killed each other in a fight. Their identification numbers may have been noted; no one worried about names. Yet Somerset men remembered how the Italian workers sang. Their music had a happy ring in the lonely stretches of wilderness.

Despite the Italian threat to the farmers' fences, the building of the extension to Kineo was good news. Anyone with a good horse could hire out to pull dumpcarts, road plows, and drags. And there appeared to be enough work to last some time, for the way up the Austin was proving more difficult than many had anticipated.

The job had been bid by J. W. Whitten & Company, a big outfit with experience in railroad construction. Mr. Charles, the construction superintendent, quickly realized that his company had underbid. A penalty clause in the contact stipulated that the company would forfeit any equipment on the job if it quit before completion. The superintendent wired his home office that the cheapest way out was to abandon the operation at the start. Mitchell & Johnston of Oakland took over, and the Somerset's new trackage inched along.

The task of clearing the right-of-way was farmed out to small jobbers, who were paid by the mile with the wood they cut thrown in. The swampers left a roadway of stumps, and their progress was marked by columns of smoke from burning brush. The blasting of cuts was also jobbed out whenever possible, each cut taking the name of the man who held the subcontract (for instance, the Mabry's cut just south of Gulf Stream Trestle). Blasting ledge was slow business. The holes for the powder charges were drilled by hand to a depth of six inches

A temporary trestle under construction above Bingham.
This became known as "Harry's Trestle" after Harry Baker, who owned
the farm being crossed by the Somerset's new extension.
RAYMOND L. FOLGER LIBRARY

below the intended roadbed. The shattered rock was removed with pickaxes, shovels, and two-wheeled dumpcarts that hauled the debris to the next point where fill was needed. It was dangerous work. Three Italians were badly hurt digging out a dynamite cartridge from the frozen ground. The cartridge exploded, blinding the men and leaving their faces swollen beyond recognition.

Blasting, digging, filling . . . the roadbed was slowly cut into the side of the mountain. It was a shelf from which you could look down on the tops of pointed spruce and the twisting blue and silver Austin. Deep ravines had been cut by brooks flowing down the mountainside, and these were spanned with trestles made from timber cut nearby. Crossing such trestles perched high in an engine cab, there seemed nothing between you and the plunge below. Eventually massive granite culverts were constructed and these temporary trestles filled. The fact that the old roadbed is still in use now, sixty years after the rails were removed, is largely due to the original engineering and the labors that went into these culverts. It is worth going down the steep side of the old fills to take a look. Patches of sunlight and shade flicker over the stone portal. A mountain brook splashes from one pool to the next and then ripples over the floor of the long granite passageway.

Today we would call such construction "labor intensive." It was only ninety-odd years ago, yet photos taken of the Somerset's construction remind us that we are living in a different age. It is hard for us to comprehend how or why men worked as hard as they did. "We worked a long day," one Italian crew boss remembered, "and then the ties would be brought up to the end of the track, and we would lay them out by lantern light ready for the next day." (The Knox family cut and hewed many of the ties for this section of the new line. They had camps along the right-of-way and were experts with a big tie ax.) For many of the immigrants the only alternatives were worse. "You are an ungrateful lot," Dominic Susi chastised one riotous crew. "Didn't I meet you at the boat in Boston and bring you up here and out of starvation?"

In contrast to making the roadbed, filling and ballasting were mechanized operations. Steam shovels were employed in the several pits from which the gravel was extracted, and the unloading of the gravel cars was done with a plow. (The sources of gravel included Owen's Pit just below Bingham Heights; Kendalls, a mile north of Deadwater; a site above Moxie Lake; and the Somerset pit near Somerset Junction.) At each pit a cable was laid over the floors of the coupled platform (flat) cars. One end of the cable was fastened to a plow positioned on the rear end of the last car. The other end was attached to the engine. When the gravel train reached the section to be ballasted or filled, the engine was uncoupled and ran ahead, pulling the plow and spilling the loads as it went.

As the tracks neared Deadwater, the reverse curves tightened and the track hugged the side of the mountain more closely. Just below Deadwater, the track rounded the last projecting cliff. A granite-block retaining wall had to be built to keep the roadbed in place. It was a sixty-foot drop to the black pools and foaming eddies of the Austin.

Some years after the road was built, the down passenger train had made its stop for a brake test at Deadwater and was getting under way when there came the sickening jar of derailed wheels dropping onto the ties. The conductor grabbed the signal cord as the car lurched, expecting at any moment to topple over the retaining wall. When they stopped, the car was leaning over the drop-off. There is no record that the conductor left his job, but the thought must have crossed his mind.

Above the retaining wall the Austin made a horseshoe loop that necessitated two major operations: A channel had to be cut across the base of this meander to divert the stream, and a large cut made for the track. Material from the cut was used in diverting the Austin, and a narrow-gauge track was built from the cut down to the stream. Carts loaded with gravel and rock were eased down, emptied, and hauled back with horses. Shans Franklin, an in-law of the Susi family, was put in charge of this operation and lost three carts in one day. Dominic was not pleased. When the job was done, the track crossed the old streambed, rounded one last turn, and arrived at Deadwater. A gateway to Maine's green gold had been opened.

A dam added "head" to the Austin's natural flowage. Inundated trees lost their bark and bleached white in the sun. Haines built a sawmill, and the Coburn heirs erected a company store. There was a Y for turning engines and plows. The Somerset rested.

Beyond Deadwater, what the railroad faced was not a climb but tight curves, swamps, and clay. Henry Hill's location of the railroad's path kept the Somerset's feet dry through much of Moxie Long Bog. The western shore of Moxie Pond necessitated more blasting and, in one place, a short causeway built on a curve. The grade was nearly flat but hardly straight. In one mile of track there were eight serpentine twists ranging from eight to twelve degrees of curvature. Speeds would have to be restricted to twenty miles per hour through this section. Even then there would be some squealing of wheel flanges when the Somerset began to haul Pullmans with their six-wheeled trucks to Kineo.

A year after the Somerset reached Deadwater, there was a new railhead seven miles north at Sandy, a nice spot on the shore of Moxie Pond. For a few years after the road was completed, passenger trains still stopped there. You could get a good meal for thirty-five cents.

Everyone had expected that there would be a lot of rock to blow, but few realized the problem that clay would present. Maine has many gifts from the age of glaciers, and deep beds of blue clay nearly as hard as shale are among them. Often the only way to remove the clay was to tunnel under and blow with black powder.

It was just northeast of Indian Pond that the extending Somerset came to Bog Brook and the "sink." The construction crews working south from Rockwood had been stopped by this obstacle for a month. Tons of fill had simply

**Engine No. 6 on newly laid track south of Deadwater.
Here the Somerset's path was blasted from the rugged hillside high
above Austin Stream.** AUTHOR'S COLLECTION

disappeared beneath the covering ooze of mud. Finally a cribwork of logs was built. As this sank, additional cribwork was added until, at a depth of twenty feet, the base seemed stable enough to lay track across the top. When train traffic was opened, however, the cribwork again sank under its weight. This sink was a constant problem; trackage was relocated in 1908, but one sinkhole still could not be avoided. The trains slowed to five miles per hour as they passed the yellow caution lanterns. Everyone who knew had an uneasy feeling when riding across the bog, especially on a night when rafts of fog drifted across the waste. Men in the locomotive cabs knew that on either side was enough mud to swallow an engine whole.

71

The Canadian Pacific built a handsome stone overpass, and the Somerset trains passing below the trans-Canada rails soon smudged the arched portal with coal smoke. Schemes for expansion lingered. In 1905 the Somerset had been authorized to extend to Chesuncook Lake and bring lumber and pulp from the Penobscot watershed to the mills on the Kennebec. In 1907 it was granted the right to run north to Seboomook at the head of Moosehead Lake and then swing westward to Canada, the promised land. The Great Northern Paper Company—with its new mill in Madison and large holdings north of Seboomook—must have been interested in this venture. But the Somerset's days of expansion were over. In 1906 it had reached its final destination at Kineo Station, 90.6 miles from Oakland.

For those who had contrived to push the railway northward from Bingham, everything was on schedule and the business looked good. In March 1906 the *Kennebec Journal* reported that three double-headers had been put over Otis Hill in one day: "With business this good, they [the railway] should be able to pay four cents on some of their stock." In 1907 the railway hauled 268,231 tons of freight and 110,935 passengers. By 1910 the figures had risen to 315,816 tons and 120,000 passengers. It was not unusual for the Somerset to deliver eighty cars a day to the Maine Central and another twenty to the Canadian Pacific. It was time for the Maine Central to take control.

When the Maine Central assumed the management of the Somerset in 1911, the vice president and chief accountant descended on Oakland to have a look at the railway's books. Horace Greeley, the Somerset's accountant, brought them out—a ledger, a day book, and a cash account.

"That's it," Greeley said when he noticed the questioning glances. Mr. Hobb, the Maine Central's accountant, began by asking a series of questions and ended by losing his patience. "Mr. Greeley, you don't know the first thing about running a railroad," he exploded.

"Maybe not," Greeley replied, "but, by gad, we know how to sell one."

PART II

≡

Life
Along the Somerset

A circus parade on the main street in Madison.
AUTHOR'S COLLECTION

Chapter Six

❧

ROUND TRIP
FOR A DOLLAR

Train schedules plainly announced that all times were subject to unavoidable delays. If you had to wait, you could while away a few minutes examining the Forepaugh Circus poster. For years one of these posters was pasted on an inside wall of the Bingham freight shed. It not only was large and colorful but held a wealth of details and character.

Across the sheet a high-wheeled engine, painted green with gold boiler bands, streaked toward a destination of thrills. The yellow coaches that followed were emblazoned EXCURSION TRAIN in fancy script. Letters on the end of each cross tie spelled out TIES THAT BIND THE PUBLIC TOGETHER. It was evident that some of the public, poor souls that they were, had missed the train. Beside the right-of-way streamed a multitude of characters, all hurrying as if there had been a gold strike. Grandpa, his forked white beard streaming in the wind, stood leaning over the dashboard of his wagon urging the horses to a faster gallop. Grandma leaned precariously over the tailgate waving a pink parasol and encouraging the stragglers. Clearly the train was going to get to the big show first. A billboard close to the road wisely advised folks to go see their depot master and buy a round-trip ticket. The banner at the top of the poster proclaimed CHEAP EXCURSION. This was not exactly honest advertising, for a round-trip fare from Bingham to the circus was $1.75.

But what a show it was! In 1890 the "4 Paw" was featuring Eclipse the trapeze horse, a vivid depiction of Custer's last stand, the crack-shot Prairie Girls, a black charger ridden in the hippodrome in a dust-raising reenactment of Sherman's famous ride, and, on top of all this, "one thousand costly animals." The ad in the paper showed Eclipse jumping from trapeze to trapeze as if spirited by Lydia Pinkham's vegetable compound (whose praise filled the next column).

75

The Somerset ran special trains to the 4 Paw and to P. T. Barnum's three-ring show when it came to Waterville. The coaches were standing room only by the time they reached Oakland and humming with excited anticipation. Wait till you see Barnum's "wonderful museum" and that troop of royal stallions. You know what they cost–$150,000! Jack Holloway, the English clown, will be there; so will that spellbinder Miss Kate Stokes, the bareback rider. And have you heard, Charlie Fish, "Champion of the World," will give his yearly salary to any man who can floor him–$50,000, if you can believe such a figure!

There was an epidemic of diphtheria in the valley when Barnum's show arrived in 1887; still the special trains ran, and the crowds were large. You might catch the disease, but at least you would see "the Greatest Show on Earth" before you died.

While you had to travel to Waterville or Bangor to see the big shows, lesser circuses did go to the smaller towns–not in special trains but with a few old made-over coaches and several boxcars. The old photograph at the beginning of this section shows a circus parade up the main street from Madison's railroad yard. Leading the menagerie is the bandwagon with its gilded Roman legionnaires and painted panels. The wagon driver is bedecked with a spiked Prussian helmet. Beside him is a man topped with a round derby; he may be the owner or the ringmaster or both. Two drummers with bearskin hats ride the backseat, and facing them are an equal number of cornetists wearing Civil War caps. Following the wagon comes an exotic assortment of men, women, and animals. One man seems to be dressed as George Washington, but like a badly mixed metaphor he is riding on a donkey that sports a cowbell around its neck. Perhaps the woman with the darker complexion will be reading futures, and certainly the big fellow with the bulging biceps will be challenging all the local heroes to try a round. The streets are crowded with townspeople following along to the field where the tent will be pitched.

Even Bingham folks got to see some wonderful sights without leaving town. There's a story about one of the village inebriates who was sitting on a baggage wagon watching a small circus unload. A long-legged animal came down the ramp from an old made-over baggage car. It braced its legs against the cleats and stiffened its knobby knees.

"Wonder how that horse broke his back," the fellow mumbled.

"That's a camel, not a horse," corrected an excited boy who had overheard.

"Well, it ain't my horse anyway," was the philosophical reply.

A show might resemble poor Hannibal reduced to his last elephant, but it was a small miracle to see a camel in Bingham. Not so many years later a boy or girl growing up in Bingham would not have this opportunity. By the 1930s and 1940s traveling shows had increasingly become something called carnivals.

The same internal combustion engine that propelled the first car through Madison in 1904 powered the rides and provided the carnival people with transportation from town to town. It is superficial to single out one agent in the complex human and technological interactions that were transforming the social and communal world along the Somerset and everywhere in rural America, but it must be said that the automobile made a profound impact. In a short space of time—their fates sealed ultimately by the Great Depression—the traveling circus and the passenger train would become rarities. Only a few of the big fairs have survived in Maine.

In 1907 the *Somerset Reporter* observed that "nearly everyone in Bingham was going to the fair in Waterville." This was an exaggeration, of course, but the

This horse-drawn wagon, photographed at a Congregational Church field day in Bingham, is the mode of transportation that the Somerset Railroad largely replaced. Its sign reads, "Hundred and sixty-one years old. The first wagon on the Kennebec River." AUTHOR'S COLLECTION

fairs drew a crowd. Pearl Woodard, the station agent at Bingham, sold 250 tickets to Embden Fair in one morning. Each of these gatherings had its specialty, and for Embden it was ox and horse pulling. Jake Miller's team of oxen hadn't cost the price of a stallion in Barnum's show, and Jake wore a flannel shirt rather than Prince Albert and top hat, but it was surely a sight to see the man sweat, swear, and spit down at Embden Fair. Jake did most of his swearing under his breath, but his oxen heard and put their necks into the yoke and moved the granite slabs until the ground underneath the drag smoked.

For people along the Somerset, Skowhegan Fair became easier to get to after a trolley line was constructed from Norridgewock to Skowhegan. The electric line carried freight as well as people, and in a cooperative venture the traction company (trolley line) and the railroad hauled stock, produce, and articles for exhibition at the fair for less than half fare. For the upper Kennebec, Skowhegan's tryst was the queen of fairs. To take a blue ribbon for a quilt or cake at Skowhegan was to have arrived. There were shows in the evening and horse races all day long and long sheds of displays and tents where the ladies of the Methodist Church fed the hungry multitude. It was at such fairs—and especially at the flower displays—that you realized most acutely the civilizing role women play in this fragile thing we call civilization.

Its timetables indicate that by 1906, the Somerset was running eight passenger trains and nine freights every weekday. What the timetables do not show is the number of special trains that were a regular occurrence in season. Every Sunday afternoon during the summer, for instance, there was a train to the North Anson Trotting Park. Later generations flock to stock-car races, avidly attend mud-runs where vehicles with big tires thrash through the slop, or fill their yards with vehicles upon which they plan to tinker, but at the turn of the century the "in" thing was the fast horse and sulky race.

From July to October you could take the Sunday-afternoon excursion train to Kineo Station, then connect with a Coburn steamboat for a cruise on the big lake. Evidently such an adventure was not considered a violation of the Sabbath, for the trip became popular with church and Sunday school groups. A much more expensive jaunt was offered with connections to Portland (where there were more people who could afford it): For twenty-five dollars you could enjoy a long weekend at the Kineo House, including train and boat fares, lodging, two dinners, two breakfasts, and a luncheon.

When the blueberries were ripe on Bald Mountain, special excursions were run from Oakland to Troutdale Station. Fifty to a hundred passengers climbed aboard equipped with ten-quart pails. One particularly nice Sunday, Reed Hilton

Excursions on Moosehead were popular and often featured a live band.
This vessel is the *Katahdin,* flagship of the Coburn steamboats.
CLIFF SAWYER COLLECTION

The Sunday Special passing Mayfield Crossing on the way to Deadwater and
Moosehead Lake. The fireman aboard was cooperating with the photographer
by making sure there was plenty of black smoke. AUTHOR'S COLLECTION

and a friend joined the expedition. They filled their pails in a couple of hours, hid them under a bush, and went off to gallantly aid several young ladies. When they returned to their cache, they found a bear had helped himself and squashed their pails in the process.

In contrast to such encounters with nature in the North Woods, excursions to Lakewood promised to put you in touch with the supernatural. The special ran to Madison, where you could connect to Lakewood via the cars of the Somerset Traction Company. In later years Lakewood was to become a successful summer theater, but in the days of the Somerset, the Spiritualists gathered there. Throngs joined them to hear the knockings and the whisperings that filled a big barn on the shores of Wesserunsett Lake. This excitement was part of the Spiritualism that swept through the upper Kennebec Valley. For a time it was a major movement in which extremists burned their Bibles. Perhaps this phenomenon was not as extraordinary as it now seems. To some considerable extent, it could be said, the mainline churches have but spread a white cloth over older rocks of occult belief.

For fifty years the Somerset's excursions, round trip for a dollar and often much less, were an integral part of life along its tracks. People marked their calendars with the date when they would forget work and get away. The Up-River Field Day held for the employees of the Great Northern was for many such an event. The special train picked people up all along the line and delivered them to the wharf at Rockwood. There the *Twilight* would be waiting, with Captain Sawyer

A Fraternal Order arrives at Kineo Station and marches to the hotel.

or Wink Merservey at the helm, to take the crowd to Seboomook. Under a large tent six hundred were fed a spread from beans to watermelon. There would be bateau races, crosscut-saw contests, a baseball game, and a children's parade.

Besides the special excursions, groups used the regular trains. In 1898 one hundred citizens from Madison rode down to Augusta to see the soldiers off. In 1910 forty-two high school seniors traveled to Washington, D.C. Those words on the "4-Paw" circus poster, "ties that bind the public together," seem factual.

All of these special trains and excursions were part of the life of the communities and part of their color and pageantry. Masonic lodges gathered by hired train to hold special convocations, and Knights Templar from their Commandries gathered to parade with their white-plumed *chapeaux* ruffled by the lake breeze. Most colorful of all, and certainly the most raucous, were the arrival of Boston's William Tell Club for its annual blowout at Spencer Bay and the pulling in of the Boston Company of Ancient and Honorable Artillery for their convention at the Kineo Hotel. By columns and companies with flying banners, these groups would fill the yard at Rockwood. A band would play, and the launch from the hotel would fire its twelve-gauge cannon. When the Appalachian Club of Boston came to Moosehead, it traveled on a train with seven special cars—sleepers, parlor cars, and a diner.

And then after so few years, all this came to an end.

Solon station agent William Soper seated in his 1905, one-cylinder Cadillac.
AUTHOR'S COLLECTION

Chapter Seven

❧

WHEN DEPOTS HAD MASTERS

THERE WAS MUCH THAT was pleasant about the Somerset's depots. Hip roofs, wide overhangs, and bay windows from which the station master could see up and down the tracks were common features, but there were many variations–an outside wainscot of vertical sheathing, perhaps, or an entablature of variegated shingles. The carpenters modified whatever standard plans there were to fit local needs. Deadwater's depot, for instance, had a full dormer with enough room for the station master to live. At one time the schoolmistress occupied the room over the station. When the train crews noticed that there was no screen on her window, they took to throwing odds and ends into her room whenever the window was open. (Boys will be boys, she decided.)

In the early days the railway's stations appear to have been painted according to local tastes or the availability of paint. Just after the turn of the century, the stations were badly in need of paint, and the railway got a good buy on a boxcar red that was generally applied to its property. This batch had a strong dose of yellow ocher that became more apparent as time went on. Later, under the Maine Central regime, the standard two tones of green were applied uniformly from Oakland to Kineo.

Bingham started with a combination depot but soon acquired a separate passenger station. It had a center bay window, and the ticket office substantially separated the waiting room into two halves, one for women, the other for men. There were two ticket windows as well. The decorations and furnishings were spartan: a potbellied stove (placed on the women's side), several wooden settees, oil lamps with large globes hanging from the ceiling, and a couple of spittoons in the men's half. A patriotic American Express sign hung on the wall along with

83

the Maine Central's schedule and the Grand Trunk's connections for points west. Such depot fixtures varied little up and down the line.

If you wanted an image of a small, efficient railroad station, it would be Solon's combination depot. Combination freight-passenger stations were built with the same division of space that Yankees used to build their farm buildings–small house, big barn. Solon's depot was narrow in width, long in length, and had a gable roof. The office with its bay window separated the small waiting room from the larger freight shed. There was a two-holer in a neat shed attachment on the rear. Adding a touch of class was the separate awning built over the southern end of the platform.

Around 1969 the Maine Central hired the Solon Volunteer Fire Company to burn this depot. As a station–in fact, as a building–it was already gone. The waiting room door was permanently jammed open, and the ridgepole sagged as if it carried the weight of too many winters. Sunlight through the jagged holes in the shingled roof made playthings of the floating dust. Rain coming in had warped the pine sheathing in the office while outside the overhang slouched onto decaying braces.

In 1905 depot master William Soper liked to park his new one-cylinder Cadillac beside the platform awning where everyone could see it. This car was the first in Solon, and Bill drove with goggles and leather gauntlets. Like so many station agents along the Somerset, he was an unusual man. Perhaps it was the constant dealing with people, the range of responsibilities, and the kaleidoscope of experiences that called such men to be depot masters. There was challenge in good weather and bad. The depot master manhandled the freight, ran the express business, kept the books, shoveled snow, washed lamp chimneys, managed the train yard (where there was one), and served as the Western Union telegrapher. You might add he was the keeper of the seal. Accountable for a good deal of money, he sent off the receipts each week sealed in wax impressed with the station's brass stamp. The pay was thirty-five to forty dollars a month.

In the days when Bill Soper was at Solon, the station clock seemed to have too few hours. In season the Northern Maine Packing Company would be canning corn–"fancy corn," it advertised, "Family Pride," "Sweet Pearl," and "Morning Glory." This meant it was time for Soper to dust off the *Pathfinder's Guide*. He usually had to consult the guide twice for each shipment–once when he made out the billing and again when the canning company complained about the costs.

The world of the agent was not as small as his office would lead you to think. He worked within a complex network of rail and car rental companies

The hotel "hack," or carriage, and a collection of passengers wait
for the train at Solon. Beyond the station is the factory where the Northern
Maine Packing Company canned its "Pride of Maine" brand fancy sugar corn.
ROBERT LORD COLLECTION

connected across the country. There were bound to be problems. For example, there was the carload of screens that got lost somewhere out on the old Portland & Rochester. The Solon station agent was involved in a hefty correspondence over this, but the car was never tracked down.

The depot master was also placed in an exposed position between the railroad and its customers. Much has been written on the noble yeomanry and honest character of the New England farmer and his wife. It is also true that the pair could be small and sometimes nasty. Sometimes the station agent got to see too much of the latter side. One agent was weighing several sacks on the scales when one toppled. Out spilled a miserable tumble of small potatoes.

"You're not going to sell these, are you?" the agent blurted.

The farmer was down on his knees scooping up the potatoes. "Just weigh them," he grunted.

Nothing was better calculated to bring out the worst in a farmer than freight rates. Take rates on shipping hogs. If a farmer shipped one pig, it automatically weighed five hundred pounds. A charge for three hundred pounds was made for each additional hog up to twenty. Hog number twenty weighed two hundred whether it liked it or not. This was obviously a sliding scale, but most farmers

85

didn't have more than a couple of hogs to ship at any one time, and it all looked rigged for the profit of the damned railroad.

The successful agent was the one who was able to do his job and remain, for the most part, friendly with his neighbors. Moses M, the Somerset's first agent at North Anson, was such a man. His full name was Moses Christopher Columbus Thompson. His neighbors preferred "Moses M," which was sufficient to distinguish him from Red Moses and Black Moses (you could keep them straight by the color of their beards) and Old Moses, the patriarch of all the Thompsons and the man who kept the tavern at the Solon Ferry—a yellow block of a building commandingly situated above the Kennebec. It was said that this senior Moses had six hundred dollars or more just drawing interest in the bank and more cattle than anyone else around. After a long life of driving cattle to Canada, passing out liquor through the wicker window in his tavern, and farming, Old Moses was drowned in the Kennebec—which unlike the Red Sea never parted for anyone.

Moses M was also a character. Like many others, he had been to California and back. He was a practical surveyor and had helped to lay out the Somerset during its early construction. He had a wife, Samantha, whom he claimed always shrank his shirts: "Take a look at them sleeves. I bought this shirt new last Wednesday. Now, I said, 'Samantha, see if you can shrink that.' And by the Lord Harry, I stood right there and watched this shirt gather."

He kept a pet raccoon in his cellar and liked to tell how the critter would take after his wife. The animal went too far when it bit Moses M. Moses always had some story going. He'd tug on his sleeves and start in talking as he wrote out your ticket.

"Ed Haskell came down early this morning for a load of grain. Had his earflaps up and those big ears of his hanging out and as red as two beets. I said to him, 'Ed, don't you know how cold it is this morning? Why in common sense don't you pull them earflaps down?' 'Well,' says Ed, 'I did have them down snug, and coming down through town a fellow asked me if I wanted a drink, and I didn't hear him.' " That was an old story, but Moses could tell it so you'd laugh again.

Not all the depot masters were as good at public relations as Bill Soper and Moses M. Hotbox Stackpole, station agent in Oakland, is remembered as having a squinty eye and smoking a cigar you could smell a mile upwind.

A large sign nailed up on the side of the station listed the dire consequences for loitering. As far as Hotbox was concerned the sign was intended especially for boys, and periodically he would call in Constable Bert Hersom to run them off the station grounds. Bert couldn't run very fast, but just to have called him was an act of war. There were retributions. A hay rake got tied to the rear of a westbound Pullman, and to top that, Stackpole arrived at his depot one morning to find a dizzy cow standing spread-legged on the nearly level roof of the freight shed. The cow had to be lowered the same way it had been raised, swinging from the freight crane. The Somerset, by the way, ran on ingenuity as much as anything else. One of the boys who raised this cow went to work for the railroad a few years later. He started as an engine wiper and ended as chief clerk.

All depot masters on the Somerset had moments of unpopularity. Elizabeth Thompson, later Mrs. Pearl Woodard, went to work for the Somerset in 1911 when she was seventeen. "A railroad is no place for a woman" was the pronouncement of George Foster, then superintendent, but Elizabeth was persistent, capable, and needed. Foster hired her as a clerk. By the time she attained the position of station master, she'd been threatened by a crazy man who promised to break her neck. However, only one of the Somerset's agents died a violent death.

Embden was a combination station much like Solon in design. It was built on ground donated by O. H. McFadden, a Somerset supporter, with the stipulation that Embden would always have a station. By 1920 the future of the Embden depot was in question. Asa Entreken was the depot master. He was seventy years old and lived in the back of the station, where he looked after the mail and what little wayfreight came and went. There was speculation that when Entreken could no longer look after things, the station would be closed.

Late on a gray Thursday afternoon in November, a Mr. Chase (who lived down the road) heard Entreken yell, "Get out of here!" The shout was followed by what sounded like the whacks of a club and the barking of a dog. Chase figured that the station agent was having a dispute with a stray dog. But as Chase sat milking, he grew more and more bothered by what he had heard. He telephoned the station and got no answer. Chase then went down to the station and discovered a bloody scene. Old Entreken was dead. His body had been dragged to the back room and wrapped in a bedspread. The down train had passed, and the mailbag thrown from the baggage car lay in a pool of blood on the platform. Chase called the sheriff.

On his way to the scene, the sheriff passed three young strangers—two riding bicycles and a third walking. The law officer paid little attention and hurried on to Embden Station. He was back on the road an hour later; there were questions he wanted to ask those three strangers. The bicycles were found in a clump of bushes near the North Anson Trotting Park. By late evening the sheriff had his

A drawing of Embden Station, where Asa Entreken met his violent end.
WALTER MACDOUGALL

suspects. At first the three young men maintained that they had come north to find work in the woods, and had tried the North Anson Manufacturing Company without luck. (This was true. Jobs were hard to get.

According to the newspaper, upon continued questioning the three suspects finally confessed to the murder and described what had taken place. They were James Purcell of New Bedford, John Brown of Boston, and Homer Spurloch from Ashland, Kentucky. After leaving the factory, they'd stolen the bicycles from outside North Anson Academy and gone north to Embden Station. At about six o'clock in the evening Agent Entreken had made two trips from the depot office to the back of the station with ashes from the stove. During the second trip, Spurloch, who had been hiding by the corner of the building, attacked the old man with a sled stake. Brown had joined the struggle wielding a knife, cutting the agent on the shoulder. The cause of death was found to be massive fractures of the skull. The youngest of the three, Purcell, had evidently held back during the killing.

The young thugs were taken to the county jail at Skowhegan. At that time splitting wood was one of the chores given to prisoners, and Spurloch and Brown smuggled an ax into their cell. Another inmate warned the jailkeeper in time. On February 17, 1921, Spurloch and Brown were found guilty of murder and sentenced to life imprisonment. Purcell was found guilty but with a recommendation for clemency.

While being placed in Entreken's kind of peril was a remote possibility, many depot masters felt they deserved hazardous-duty pay. At Bingham, before the advent of town water, the engine tank was filled from a walled spring (Station Agent Pearl Woodard kept a trout here until it mysteriously disappeared). A small shingled building housed the boiler which furnished steam for the pump and for keeping water from freezing in winter. Few railroad employees visited the pump house because Ed Fogg, the pumpman, kept a pet snake there; it would twine itself around Fogg's arm and flick its tongue at anyone who stopped to talk.

Fogg once had trouble with a tooth and took a day off to go down to the dentist in North Anson. He made arrangements with Olaf, a Swede, to fire the pump boiler. Olaf was a conscientious fellow who spent his days shoveling bituminous into the large loading tubs on the coaling yard. Olaf tried very hard to do both jobs this day, but on his last trip to the pump house, he found that the steam pressure had dropped so low that he could not activate the inspirator in order to get more water into the boiler. His knowledge of steam equipment was rudimentary, but he knew that this was an unhealthy situation. He ran for the station propelled with the fear of exploding boilers. Excitement didn't help Olaf's English, but Agent Woodard finally got the drift of what had happened.

The problem was a new one for the station agent, but he quickly decided that what was left of the fire should be raked out. Halfway through the operation, a shovel fell over against the upright boiler. Olaf yelled, "She blow!" and was gone through the open door, leaving Woodard to calm his nerves and finish the job.

Pearl Woodard came to Bingham in 1911, when the previous station master was fired for leaving an important group of passengers treading the morning snow outside a locked station door. Pearl stayed at the post until he retired in 1945. Thus he saw the railway's grand days as well as the closing of the extension to Kineo and the demise of passenger service. Pearl was a survivor—short, physically tough, and bright. When he teamed up with John Hughes, the telegraph lineman, no one around could beat them at horseshoes. Pearl's special talent with figures and his memory made him devastating at cards as well. A number of the "city boys" got a real shock when they sat down to play with Pearl Woodard. Of course, his ability with figures and his recall also made Pearl valuable to the railroad. He was a character and in many ways the quintessential depot master.

When a new rookie agent at Deadwater got into a tangle with his accounts, the superintendent asked Pearl to go up and straighten the mess out. The next evening Woodard took his oldest son, Clint, and headed up the grade to Deadwater on a pumpcar. The new agent was a tall, lanky fellow with a pimply complexion. Pearl had his doubts, but he launched into a lesson on bookkeeping. The young fellow sat looking out the window and working with his face. Whenever Pearl asked for a particular ledger or pile of papers, the new agent jumped up, knocked his head soundly on the station semaphore handles—sixty pounds of iron bolted to the wall—and without a wink fetched what was required. The only emotion he showed that whole evening was upon hitting his shin against an open desk drawer. That time he bent over rubbing his leg and moaning as though his bone had been broken in three places.

Pearl was feeling no sympathy by the time the session ended. Clint sat in the corner trying to smother his giggles every time the agent hit his head on the semaphore handles.

"Now, do you know anything that I told you?" Pearly asked at last.

The lanky frame eased back farther into the desk chair, and there began an astonishing recapitulation. Step by step, column by column, every detail was given back. The new agent was a wonder!

M. C. R. R. Station, Oakland, Me.

A postcard showing the Maine Central Railroad station at Oakland, circa 1910.

Pearl Woodard.

Pearl soon found that the position of depot master in Bingham was actually two jobs. By giving him a clerk as a helper, the railroad expected that Pearl would be able to run the stations and yard at Bingham while he was also operating the small passenger station at Bingham Heights. At best this meant a workday starting at five A.M. and ending late in the evening. Pearl bought a bicycle and began pedaling back and forth between his two posts.

Three passenger trains a day stopped at the Heights, the last at eleven o'clock in the evening. Providing the bicycle's front wheel didn't find a perverse rut, it was a welcome relief to coast down from the Heights into the village. The

The old Somerset line looked like this when it was first put through to Bingham Heights. This is engine No. 2 with a full complement of two passenger cars and one baggage car. A box car served as the station at this time, circa 1908. MINA TITUS SAWYER COLLECTION

streets would be empty under the quiet elms. The town's electrical company turned off the power at nine-thirty, and the houses were in darkness as Pearl made his way home.

When his finances improved, Pearl retired the bicycle and bought a Model T truck. As a result he began to put on weight—nothing alarming until one morning at Bingham Heights. Even with a light load the baggage wagon pulled hard; piled with several trunks and an assortment of suitcases and express boxes, one wagon could require three men. Pearl took off his coat and rolled up his sleeves. While loading the baggage, he bent over to pick up a tag that had come loose—and the seat of his pants gave way. There were several women behind him, and they began to giggle through hands raised ineffectually over their mouths. Pearl's face turned red enough to have flagged the train. He backed up to the station wall, worked his way to the waiting room door, and ducked into the office. It was as bad as he feared. The whole seat was gone, and his shirt was flapping out like the tail of a deer going over a fence.

Pearl made a ritual of checking the toilet door before locking up the station. Tramps were common, and the toilet was a good place to hide. One afternoon he found the toilet door locked from the inside. He knocked, announced that he was about to close the station, and then stepped out on the platform to avoid any embarrassment. After a decent length of time he returned. The door was still locked. There was a space between the toilet partition and the ceiling. Pearl got a stepladder, climbed up, and looked down into the cubicle. It was empty. There was also a space between the toilet door and the floor. Obviously, whoever had slipped the lock bolt had crawled out under the door–a gap of less than eight inches but space enough for a boy. Still, Pearl couldn't remember there being any boys around that afternoon; in fact, there had been very few passengers.

A few days later a trim little lady with white hair and a large cameo brooch under her chin came into the station. When there no one was in the waiting room, she approached the ticket window.

Things got busier in Bingham Heights when the new station house was built. Here, engine No. 7–a high-wheeled 4–4–0–and train No. 15 are headed for Kineo.

"You must have the lock on that door fixed. It sticks," she said, jabbing the point of her umbrella at the toilet door.

A smile that should have remained hidden spread over Pearl's face and despite his best efforts turned to a laugh. The little lady was already furious.

Occasionally Pearl got a chance to go hunting. He had been on such an expedition just north of the Gulf Stream Trestle and was walking homeward down the tracks in the twilight when he heard the labored exhaust of a freight train working its slow way up the grade. As the engine passed, Pearl pulled out a large handkerchief and tied it bandit-fashion around his face. When the caboose rattled by, he swung onto the rear steps and poked his rifle through the door.

"This is a stickup," he hissed.

The conductor was putting a frying pan on the stove; it clattered to the floor. The brakeman's face went white. For a moment no one moved. Then Pearl stepped back and swung off the rear. No one appeared at the caboose's open door.

The next morning when the freight backed into Bingham Yard, the brakeman motioned Pearl into a corner.

"Don't say a word to anyone," the brakeman whispered, "but we were held up last night."

Pearl thought it best to act surprised. "What happened?"

"Nothing, we scared the fellow off."

"Good work," Woodard said, slapping the brakeman on the back.

Slow-moving trains came close to getting Pearl into serious trouble. The agent at Troutdale Station once sent out an emergency call for three cans of Prince Albert tobacco. Pearl got the tobacco and tied the three cans into a bundle along with a note stating their destination. It would be simple to pass the package to one of the rear-end crew when the next freight pulled past Bingham Heights. There was no evidence of life in the buggy when the next train rolled past the station platform, though. Pearl heaved the cans through an open window.

The minute he saw the brakeman that next day, Pearl knew what had happened. The man's eye had turned a spectacular purple edged with green and yellow.

"Were you on the platform when we went by the Heights yesterday?" the man asked.

Pearl prudently gave him a blank look, then with honest concern asked what had happened.

"Some damned fool tossed three cans of Prince Albert in the window, and if I find out who it was I'll kill him."

Only two things really bothered Agent Woodard: not having time to go fishing, and lightning. As the old-timers put it, the electric storms hit Bingham Heights "desperate hard." One bolt came through the window of a house close to the depot, traveled the whole length of the garret, and then went out the other window without touching a thing. Lightning plays at mysterious games, and most of all it likes to prance around telegraph wires.

The afternoon passenger train was due at the Heights. As far as Agent Woodard was concerned, it was a race to see which would arrive first—the train or the black clouds coming down the Kennebec Valley. The train whistled for Mayfield Crossing just as the first sharp crack tossed back and forth between the hills. The moment the train pulled out, Pearl rushed into the office, sent his report, and plugged in the lightning arresters on the telegraph line. Just as he turned the key in the station door a sizzling ball, bright as ten thousand burning matches, hit the line in front of the depot and dropped to the ground. Pearl ran for his Model T and headed down the hill. That evening he found the lightning arresters blasted to pieces, with one large fragment of metal embedded in the sheathing on the other side of the office.

Summer had its lightning, and winter its wind and snow. Austin Junction, just below Bingham Yard, was a cold place where drifts crested the highest fence posts. Unfortunately, the scales for weighing freight cars were here at the Junction. An agent had to stand full in the teeth of the wind and adjust the scales with stiffening fingers. Pearl Woodard was involved in this process one bitter January morning. He stuffed the waybills into his mackinaw pocket along with his gloves; when the last car rolled off the scales, he jerked his gloves out without thinking. The air was filled with a flurry of yellow slips of paper. The waybills skittered across the crust, and Pearl went plunging after them. He finally retrieved all but one. That spring he found the missing slip frozen into the ice near the scale.

When Woodard got back to the station he thawed his hands over the stove and then sat down to the telegraph key. The railway would either build some sort of a shelter over the scales at Austin Junction or send a new depot master to Bingham. A small crew of men arrived the next day with a roll of old canvas. The shanty they built kept out the frostbite. (Later a trim little structure was built over the scales beside the weighing platform.) Still, the winter winds at Austin Junction could find their way through the heaviest long johns.

A railroad family once moved down from Moxie to civilization. Their belongings and livestock were shipped to Austin Junction in a boxcar.

"We lost a hen when we loaded," the conductor confided when he met Woodard at the weighing scales. To everyone's surprise the bird was discovered sitting rigidly on a tie-rod under the boxcar from Moxie. It had ridden twenty-three miles hobo-style, its feet clamped in a frozen grip. When Pearl suggested they get the hen loose and take it back to the station, the conductor looked at him as though he were crazy.

"Why not?" asked Pearl. "I've thawed myself out a good many times after being down here."

The hen revived in the heat of the office stove. By the time the day ended it was sitting on the agent's desk, cocking its head at the clicking telegraph.

The old depots along the Somerset were special places–environments of amplified life along the vibrating string of the railway–and the depot masters were often unusual men. Many of them had been places and done things; Pearl Woodard, for instance, was Maine born but had gotten most of his railroad training in the Midwest. When these depot masters returned and settled down, they kept trying some new adventure. A person who can read Morse code, type, and talk all at the same time has to have some special abilities honed sharp by practice. Technically the job called for accuracy in figures, a strong memory, and a quick wit in the face of the unexpected. Common to all the most successful depot masters, too, was their enjoyment of a joke and their wonderful capacity to tell a story–especially on themselves. Simply put, they enjoyed life and most people most of the time.

These men were at home in their work. The outside world came periodically to their depots. The closer world of their neighbors warmed itself at the station stoves and loaded aboard the passing trains both their commerce and the "stuff that dreams are made of."

Chapter Eight

※

SPANS OF WOOD AND STEEL

SPRING HAD COME with its usual abruptness to Maine. There was a quick transition from slush and mud to dust, all in a few weeks. It was Memorial Day 1906. The weather was unseasonably warm, with a fresh breeze ruffling the Kennebec River. The North Anson Extra had just pulled out of Anson, rumbling south through the long covered bridge toward Madison. At Anson Depot, Agent Lester Williams had finished his lunch and was catching up on his toothpicking when he heard the first shouts. He catapulted from his desk chair and rushed out onto the station platform. Someone was yelling that the railroad bridge was on fire!

One quick glance down the tracks was enough for confirmation. Even as Williams stared, a dancing line of flames, orange under the growing smoke, flickered up the shingled roof of the covered bridge. The agent rushed back to his chair, sent a rapid call for help on the telegraph, then joined the growing line of pail-carrying townsmen running toward the bridge. The fire had started close to the Anson side. It was still confined to a small patch on the roof, and having the river within such easy reach gave the bucket brigade a real advantage. Williams was optimistic that the bridge could be saved.

The Madison Volunteer Fire Company had already assembled for the Memorial Day parade. Decked out in their brand-new uniforms and full of esprit de corps, the volunteer firemen arrived quickly at the Madison end and began laying a hose line through the bridge—over five hundred feet—to the Anson end and the fire. With the hose connected to the pumper, the bucket slingers were waved aside.

Then it happened. A fresh scud of breeze darkened the river and sent a cloud of fiery fragments bouncing along the bridge's roof. The hose crew found themselves between the original fire and a new blaze, which began to eat at the

The fiery end of the covered railroad bridge spanning the Kennebec at Madison on May 30, 1906. AUTHOR'S COLLECTION

cedar shingles like sparks in a dry hay field. The firemen dropped their hose and made a running retreat back across the bridge. From then on, Williams lost hope.

Producing its own draft, the fire spread quickly. Siding boards and roof timbers plummeted in red avalanches into the Kennebec. Through rifts in the smoke, the crowd along the riverbanks caught sight of the rails, still spiked to the burning cross ties, sagging over the empty spans. The laminated arches stood to the last, but finally they, too, toppled over and went hissing into the river.

This covered bridge at Madison was the first of three such structures on the Somerset to disappear. Yet, despite the constant threat of fire, it was the only one that burned. Precautions were taken against such conflagrations. Enginemen had standing orders never to work steam through the wooden bridges, and firemen were instructed to kick shut the locomotive's dampers before the engine passed through the portals. Section crews kept the water barrels, spaced along the spans, filled, and periodically the bridge interiors were whitewashed to discourage any stray embers from starting a fire. Evidently these precautions had some effect, for all three covered bridges at least survived the era of wood-burning engines that spit out showers of sparks.

In these bridges Somerset stockholders had a big investment to protect. During the early years when the railroad was making its slow push northward, bridges contributed hugely to construction costs. Although it may sound small to modern ears, the figure of twenty thousand dollars—the cost of a wooden bridge such as the six-hundred-foot structure across the Kennebec at Norridgewock— was a major expenditure.

Maine's old wooden covered bridges were masses of timber constructed to various plans, but none stronger or more beautiful than the Town lattice selected by the Somerset. The principal support of a Town lattice is a system of criss-crossed two-by-sixes, secured at the intersections with pins of ash or oak, to form a long latticework. Somerset bridges employed two such lattices reinforcing each other on each side of the bridge.

There was no problem making a lattice-type bridge to fit any length of span. Ithiel Town of New Haven, Connecticut, who patented this design, advertised that his lattice could be "made by the mile and cut off by the yard." Another advantage to Town's bridge was that the lattice could be fabricated on the banks of the river in sections laid flat on the ground. When finished, these sections could be rolled out on temporary scaffolding and then raised into place, in much the way timber barns were raised.

The many holes required for the pins—eighteen hundred in a one-hundred-foot span—were bored with a hand-cranked machine. The operator straddled the beam, sitting on a board that formed the base of this simple apparatus, and turned two cranks powering the horizontally mounted bit before him. The gadget looked like a large iron eggbeater, but with its sharp bit the chips tumbled quickly. When the bridge's great supporting structures were completed, the rails were spiked to the cross ties, which in turn were bolted to ten-inch by ten-inch stringers. The stringers, in their own turn, were supported by ten-by-sixteen-inch cross members that formed the bridge's floor. The whole structure, fixed by pins and iron stay rods, was tremendously strong. Sheathed and roofed to keep out the weather, such a bridge might well outlast even a railroad's long-range mortgages. Yet for all the material and work and money that went into these bridges, they were far cheaper than those made of iron or steel. As late as 1890, good spruce was selling for only eighteen dollars per thousand board feet.

At Norridgewock the true beauty of the Town lattice bridge was hidden behind completely sheathed sides. To save on the cost of building high masonry piers, the tracks were run over the roof of the bridge. This railroading on a ridge-pole had its dangers. Swinging from a car, a man needed to watch his step, particularly when winter brought a coating of ice. As one old railroader remembers, the Norridgewock bridge "sort of left a feller up in the air and out in the open." On one occasion a flatcar went off the bridge and plunged down to the frozen river. The splintering crash could be heard throughout Norridgewock village.

The bridge across the Kennebec at Madison was another Town lattice structure reaching some 512 feet in five spans. This time the trains went through the bridge as if in a very long, very narrow barn. Despite the enmity between Madison and Anson over the former town's lack of financial support for the railroad, there was a constant stream of rail and foot traffic across this bridge between the two. Because trains couldn't stop on the bridge to throw off passengers who had no tickets, someone was always riding free over the Kennebec. One woman pedestrian got caught halfway through the bridge by a freight train, but neither she nor her baby in its perambulator was hurt. When things reached the point that wheelbarrows were being trundled across the bridge, the railroad made hard-and-fast rules against pedestrian traffic—and sometimes enforced them.

The covered bridge at North Anson was the least pretentious of the three Town lattices on the Somerset, but it was the most picturesque. At North Anson the Carrabassett River dropped over the upturned ledges between banks shaded by huge elms. The village's oldest street ran along the northern bank, crossing the tracks just in front of the bridge portal. The portals of the bridge became a kind of art-deco collage complete with posters for the circus and such commodities as "Lay-or-Bust" chicken feed.

In 1907, the year after the Madison bridge burned, the Somerset replaced the wooden span at North Anson with a practical iron bridge. While construction was under way, stages carried passengers across the road bridge and buckboards toted freight around the gap in the line. Work progressed nicely. A report that three workers fell off the new construction is not surprising, but that they did so without serious injury is remarkable. Then a spring freshet took out the centering. Watching the wreckage sweep down the Carrabassett, Gene Cook, who had the job of toting passengers around the construction, figured he had a job for life. The engineers went back to work with more respect for the stream they were trying to cross.

Trains continued to cross the high roof of the wooden bridge at Norridgewock until 1921. During these intervening years another generation or two of boys and girls had the opportunity to play inside its dark, wooden tunnel and to run the catwalk under its roof. Below, the Kennebec swept swiftly past, making it seem as if the bridge were flying upstream at a dizzying pace. Best of all was to be inside the bridge when the trains crossed above. Then the timbers creaked and shivered, and the dark cavern echoed with the roar of wheels overhead.

A Somerset freight train heads north toward Madison in a postcard of the massive covered bridge across the Kennebec at Norridgewock. The high approach to the bridge made placing the tracks on the roof a practical necessity. The bridge's "Town lattice" construction and laminated arches are hidden beneath the sheathing here, but the former is clearly visible in the photograph below, taken as the structure was dismantled.

DOWN EAST MAGAZINE COLLECTION

Yet, despite the longevity of the Norridgewock bridge and the secret pleasures of youth, it is the "through covered bridges," like those at Madison and North Anson, that the public recalled. Passengers on the trains that passed through these bridges remembered the pattern of sunbeams and shadows that played the full length of the span through openings left between the siding boards and the eaves for vent smoke. This ventilation wasn't always effective—as passengers sitting beside an open coach window often discovered—but the openings did expose the lattice and provide a tracery of light and dark.

Covered bridges might be as pleasant as a grape arbor during the day, but at night they were as dark as a cave. It was said that they were inhabited by tramps and worse. One woman remembers how as a little girl she and her mother, who played piano at local dances, would cross the street in North Anson as they walked home, in order to keep as far away as possible from the dark, staring bridge portal. One night a figure suddenly glided out of the darkness of the bridge's mouth, wearing a long white gown that the night breeze swirled into a ghostly shroud. This apparition turned out to be a neighbor trying to catch her husband on his prowls, but even so mundane and lowly an explanation could not diminish the memory of that white specter materializing out of the North Anson railroad bridge.

Wooden spans along the Somerset were the proper sounding boards for those high-wheeled locomotives—and they were something more. They added to the scene as well as being a way across the river. Somehow, they fitted the view. It was as if they were as indigenous as the Maine pine and spruce that gave them form.

When the railroad crossed the Kennebec at Solon in 1888, its bridging of rivers had entered the Iron Age. The Somerset took great pride in this new bridge at Solon. It was featured on the railway's pass for 1898. The three spans added up to four hundred feet of unattractive, flat-topped Parker truss. The view was spectacular, however. The bridge crossed at the lip of roaring Caratunk Falls, a spray-filled drop that still looked very much as it had when the Abenaki fished for salmon and shad.

By 1908 the railway had seventeen iron and steel bridges totaling 2,183 feet in length. The Austin above Deadwater was crossed with a short Warren truss, Black Brook on a 60-foot girder bridge, and the Kennebec at Indian Pond with a single-span through bridge of 194 feet. The Kennebec was getting narrower. By the time the railroad reached Kineo, concrete was being used for both culverts and one bridge with a twelve-foot arch.

The railroad had always made ample use of timber trestles. Their number rose and fell depending on whether the Somerset was on the move or the river had been rambunctious. The long trestle at Old Point, the high trestle at Jones Brook, and the curved trestle approach to the Norridgewock bridge were eventually filled.

The epithet "The Trestle" was reserved for only one structure, that steel marvel which spanned the Gulf Stream gorge. Except in high water Gulf Stream was an unpretentious brook, but it had done a great task in cutting a deep valley into the heart of a mountain. Henry Hill studied the situation, triangulating, running levels, and making calculations in his field book. There was no way around it: To preserve the grade, the tracks would have to span the Gulf at its widest point. In all New England, few trestles would compare in height or length—700 feet long and 125 feet above the streambed. It was a ribbon of steel resting on six towers. From the stream this trestle stretched overhead, a narrow band of girders and cross ties against the sky. The webbed girders gave an openness to the towers and a misleading impression of frailty.

The Boston Bridge Company began construction in 1904, hauling cement for the piers by wagon up an old tote road that ran along the edge of the Austin. By the time the track crews had laid rail to the Gulf, the tower piers were ready for the girders. Ramps of rough timber, later replaced by approaches of fill, were constructed on each side of the Gulf; beginning at the southern end and reaching out one span at a time, the trestle was extended across the gorge. A donkey crane mounted on a flatcar handled the heavy side girders. Two tall timber masts with long booms swinging from either bank eased the tower members into place. Onlookers were dubious about the whole operation, but the last span fitted perfectly into its slots. It was a nice piece of engineering.

The Somerset tested its new trestle with caution. Locomotives double heading up the grade to Deadwater were required to uncouple so that the lead engine might cross the trestle alone. Speed was restricted to ten miles an hour, a maximum limit easy enough for northbound trains to obey but a lot more difficult for those running downgrade to Bingham. By 1911, the stability of the trestle having been proven, the Somerset began running its newest ten-wheelers over the spans—engines that when fully loaded weighed some sixty tons. Still, there was a standing order that heavy wreck trains out of Waterville Yard were not to cross the trestle, and yellow "slow-order" boards remained posted at both approaches to the Gulf.

The final test of the trestle's strength came quite by accident. In 1927 a washout of the Canadian Pacific caused that road to reroute its traffic over the Somerset's tracks. One of the CP trains was the Red Wing, a crack Pullman

The Somerset built an iron bridge across the Kennebec River at Solon. It was complete in 1889 except for the last span. In the foreground, a booming economy is evidenced in the foundation for a new dam and paper mill. LAURENCE BROWN COLLECTION

The railroad was so proud of its first metal bridge that company officials splurged on the extra cost of having the structure's image printed on the Somerset's 1898 travel pass. This ticket bears the name of the Honorable A. A. Burleigh, president of the Bangor and Aroostook Railroad. AUTHOR'S COLLECTION

running from Montreal to Boston and consisting of two engines plus heavy cars. The Red Wing took the trestle one dark night in a rush of metal and flash of lighted windows. If any of the crew remembered the rule about no double-headers over the Gulf, it was too late when the train rounded the sharp curve just north of the trestle, sped down the tangent, and headed over the black abyss. The trestle held. Old-timers on the Somerset shook their heads when they heard what had happened. The general feeling around the head office was the less said about the incident, the better.

Gulf Stream Trestle could be a perilous place. Trainmen perched in the cupola of a snowplow were always relieved to have the spans behind them. Plow trains, running fast to clear the drifts from the rock cuts, hit the trestle in a cloud of flying snow. One ice-blocked rail could jettison the plow over the side to become so much kindling and scrap metal on the floor of the Gulf. A man would brace himself when the nose of the plow rounded the final curve, and ahead lay the thin band of the trestle.

Engineers never allowed themselves to dwell on the possible consequences of a mishap. Pat Hursey was at the throttle of a locomotive that lost a tire from one of its drivers midway across the trestle. Pat resisted the urge to throw the air-brake handle into emergency position and prayed instead. When he had stopped the train safely on the other side, he climbed down from the cab and settled his bulk firmly on the embankment. No one thought it strange to see tears of relief running down his cheeks.

An engineering feat and a place of sudden fear, Gulf Stream Trestle was also a vantage point from which to enjoy a panorama of scenic beauty. Below was the Gulf, and beyond opened the valley of the Austin with its glinting stream and overlapping mountains. The view from high above the Gulf was beautiful in all seasons, provided the black towers and rivet-studded girders did not remind you of the grim stories associated with the trestle itself.

Over the years the trestle claimed the lives of three men and one large black bear. The animal died one day as freight train number 49 was having its usual troubles climbing the grade to Deadwater. John Vigue was coaxing all he could out of his locomotive; the fireman was sweating; at best, it was going to be a tight haul. Then when the train swung around the curve, a bear was in the center of the trestle. The animal turned its head as John sounded the whistle but didn't budge—determined, it appeared, to sit and think things out. John was doing some figuring, too. He realized that if he hit the bear, there was a good chance the train would be derailed; if he stopped the train, he'd have to double all the way into Deadwater, and he was running late as it was. The bear relieved

Built by the Boston Bridge Company, the Gulf Stream Trestle was 125 feet high and more than 600 feet in length. Although the structure had an "airy" look, it was deceptively strong. AUTHOR'S COLLECTION

A pulp train crosses the Gulf Stream Trestle. AUTHOR'S COLLECTION

Steady nerves were a prerequisite for the painters who worked on 100-foot-high staging alongside the trestle.

John of his dilemma. It jumped from the trestle. For a number of years afterward its skeleton bleached on the rocks below, a reminder of the bone-breaking drop.

The first human tragedy at the trestle came one winter morning when two men from a lumber camp at Deadwater decided to walk the tracks to Bingham. They were halfway across the span when the southbound plow train overtook them. One of the men jumped; the other lay down, half over the side, hanging for dear life to the side stringer. The plow passed in a whirl of snow, leaving paint on the man's sleeve. After climbing back onto the deck, he ran the whole distance to Bingham for help for his comrade, but there was no need to hurry. As a result of this accident, the railroad built small "step-out" platforms at intervals across the trestle.

The second death was intentional. Again the victim was a logger from Deadwater. One Saturday night he bought a coil of rope at Whitney's Hardware Store in Bingham. The next morning a rail patrolman made his inspection before the Sunday passenger train was due. He spotted a carefully folded coat on one of the trestle's step-outs. When the coat was still there on Monday morning, the section crew investigated and found a rope tied to a brace, its free end swinging in the wind. Below was the sprawling figure of a man whose weight had been too much for the rope. The section crew hurried into the ravine to find that the poor fellow was still alive. A call from the phone in a box at the south end of the trestle brought the doctor and nurse from Bingham, both clutching tight to the seat of an overheated motorcar. The doctor stitched together a coat, which was slung on poles for a stretcher, but there was little they could do for the dying man.

Gulf Stream Trestle claimed its last life during repairs on one of the tower piers, which had been undermined by water. Bags of cement were loaded onto a section car and pushed out onto the trestle, where they could be lowered to the crew below. The job had been routine and was almost finished. The rope was secured around the last bag, and while one worker prepared to ease the cement over the side, his coworker turned to push back the empty car. As he turned, there was a cry. He whirled to see his companion disappear over the edge.

One old codger came close to being the trestle's fourth victim. It was his habit to drive his horse and wagon to Bingham every Saturday night, get his fill and more, and then rely on the horse to bring him back to his farm beside the Austin. As soon as his master had staggered out of the local bar and rolled himself onto the open tailgate, the faithful animal would start for home. It was a satisfactory arrangement until the night the horse made a wrong turn at Mayfield Crossing. It must have been a rough ride over the ties, but the snoring farmer did not awaken until the horse stopped. Instead of the familiar farmyard, there was nothing but a black hole on both sides of the wagon. The horse had stopped on the first open cross ties of the trestle.

For twenty-eight years the trestle shouldered the Somerset's traffic across the Gulf: varnished and gilded Pullmans carrying summer people from New York and Boston to Moosehead Lake and the Kineo House; coaches loaded with woods crews on their way to fell timber at Indian Pond and Bald Mountain; and special trains filled with happy excursionists on their way to pick blueberries at Moxie Pond. The cords of pulp in special rackcars destined for the Madison mills, the thousands of board feet of long logs, the tons of hay, sides of beef, gallons of spirits, and cases of Poland Spring water made a colossal tonnage.

With the railway gone, painters who had once worked from swaying staging far above the pointed tops of spruce no longer kept up their battle against the rust. Nor did the inspector cling to the webbed girders like a wind-troubled spider to test the riveted joints with his hammer. Still, the trestle lasted until 1976. Almost to its last days it carried heavily loaded log trucks across the Gulf.

PART III

The Somerset Enters the Wilderness

Lumber camp in northern Maine.

Chapter Nine

THE FORESTS
COME DOWN

THE KINGDOM OF SPRUCE and pine began at Deadwater. The rails of the Somerset opened this country, and the loggers followed. In the beginning the "earls" of Deadwater were Governor William Haines and his brother Frank. Some said that the governor put Frank in charge at Deadwater just to get him out of the way, but what people say is often unfair. The settlement grew. By 1908 there was a post office, a one-room school, and a row of houses on the hillside east of the tracks. On a still winter morning Deadwater became a place of smokes—tall columns of vapor from a dozen chimneys and the stacks of the locomotives standing tender-to-pilot on the siding.

When the wind swept over the Austin Flowage, it could be terribly cold. Reed Hilton once got sent to Deadwater to fill in for the wiper who had the flu, and small wonder the fellow was sick. The wiper's job was to keep the locomotives from freezing up during the night. It was a bitter task. In the blackness of the wind-driven cold you moved from engine to engine with a mittened hand over your face. The boardinghouse was heaven: There was plenty to eat, and you could sleep all day buried under the blankets.

There soon were other lumber barons in the settlement. The Coburns owned the township of Mayfield just to the east of Deadwater. They sold stumpage (cutting rights) to loggers like Walter Robinson of Bingham, and these successful men were soon at work. A mile above the Deadwater the Austin splits; the North Branch runs out of Austin Pond, and the South Branch flows with many small tributaries across Mayfield township. Lumberman Gene Webster, who knew his business, once stated that Mayfield had the finest timber he had ever seen. The cutting of that township began in 1906 and lasted for nine years.

During this period 113 million feet of logs were sent down the Austin to the Somerset at Deadwater. A series of dams and flowages provided and controlled the water for the drives. Going upstream, you came to Week's Basin and then Baker and Palmer Flowages. Each water reserve had its complement of mosquitoes. One man reported that he had shot two mosquitoes up at Palmer Flowage before he discovered that they weren't ducks.

In spring, when water filled these flowages, the wooden gates of the dams were opened and the drive was on. Once the landings of logs were "broken in" and started down the rolling stream, the drive never slackened. Jams were blasted or picked apart by men who had handled peaveys and pick poles from boyhood. They worked until they would fall asleep while eating their supper of beans.

Under the spring sun the logs floated into the boom at Deadwater, some to be sawed at the mill, others to be loaded onto the log bunks and brought down the railway.

Jack Hardy was a house painter who lived in Bingham. There was more in Jack's artistic soul than could be expressed with a four-inch brush. He decorated things like the stage curtain at the Grange Hall, created amazing signs, and drew cartoons. His rendition of a log train making its adventurous descent from Deadwater manages to capture a wealth of detail and make some telling commentary at the same time. Arthur Tupper is at the throttle of old number 6. From the safe vantage point of a large rock Governor John Fremont Hill, wearing a long frock coat and a derby hat, is waving his handkerchief. Beside him waving his hat stands Railway Superintendent William Ayer, who is drawn smaller than the governor. The superintendent is shouting, "Take off your hat, Governor." He is addressing not the figure next to him but Governor Haines, who sits astride the first load of logs, holding a pair of reins attached to the engine. Haines, in turn, is shouting "Hang on, Frank" to his brother, who is chained down to the next load and not talking. Behind, the log bunks buck and toss.

Bringing the logs down from Deadwater was no joke. To begin with, the only air brakes on these trains were those on the locomotive, and to end with these brakes didn't do much good. The log bunks were primitive. Each was a single four-wheeled truck with a heavy bolster upon which the logs rested. Usually two bunks were used to support a load of logs. Once the logs were chained down, they, themselves, formed a rather ridged "car." These "cars" were then connected to form a train by long wooden poles called "reaches" using the old link-and-pin couplings.

In making up such a train, one man had to take the heavy reach on his shoulder and guide it into place while a second trainman dropped the coupling

Two of the Somerset's notorious log bunks. Note the horizontal "reach,"
or arm, that protrudes into the photograph from the left. Its metal end
incorporates a hole for the coupling pin linking the bunks.
AUTHOR'S COLLECTION

pin into place. A railroader told me that a third fellow was helpful for doing the swearing. Leon Greely and another young brakeman once tried supporting the reach on a pole held between them. It seemed smarter than for one of them to slip and slide on the snow and ice between the rails manhandling a reach while the loads of logs closed overhead like the top slice of a sandwich. They got cussed out by the conductor for being yellow and slowing down the operation.

After the log train had been assembled, the real challenge began. Ahead were eight miles of downgrade. Each bunk had a set of mechanical brakes. The brake wheel stuck out from the side so as not to interfere with the load. One brakeman set these wheels while a second applied the finishing touch with a brake club, a stick thrust through the spokes of the brake wheel and used as a lever for a final twist. The conductor checked the brakes as he walked along the train toward the caboose. This was a crucial operation. On a frosty morning, brakes set too tightly would lock the wheels. If that happened, the train was in for a real toboggan ride down the mountain, with the wheels acting as sled runners. On the other hand, brakes set too loosely would lead to a runaway train.

The least-disastrous possibility was to set the brakes so tightly that the train couldn't pull out.

One winter evening Pearl Woodard rode down from Deadwater on a log train. The crew got the brakes set too tightly. Up in the cab Engineman John Vigue backed on the slack and gave several yanks without budging the train. After resetting the brakes, they got down to Bingham Heights only to get stuck again. Vigue damned the mountain and the crew with real finesse, and swore to Woodard that he would never make a log run again. It certainly seemed as if the mountain had it in for John. He once locked the drive wheels of his locomotive coming down from Deadwater and slid far enough to spot (flatten) the drivers in good shape.

To eliminate wheel locking, crews often set the brakes on the bunks while the train was in motion. They worked along the sides of the train as fast as they could. It was another tricky operation with only one chance to err in judgment: Once on the grade down to Bingham it was "Hang on, Frank" all the way. An engineer could hold back a little with the straight air brake on the locomotive, and the fireman could set the hand brake on the tender. Setting the locomotive's brakes took a special skill on the engineer's part, though. If he set too hard, then either he would lock the drivers (as Vigue had) or the log bunks would run in on the locomotive and snap a reach. The engineer could also whistle for "down brakes"—one short pull on the whistle chain. At this signal the men on the rear-end crew would set the brake on the caboose—which did about as much good as a fire extinguisher in hell. There was, of course, no way to further tighten the brakes on the bunks once the train was rolling down the mountain.

Braking a log train was a young man's job. Clinton Knight was twenty-one when he went braking on the Somerset. His run hauled forty- to sixty-foot pine and spruce logs from a cut in Moxie Gore to just below Solon, where the logs were dumped into the Kennebec. All the rest of his life Knight remembered the smell of those hot, smoking brakes. He made two trips a day, and there was plenty of opportunity for a man to age rapidly.

Arthur Tupper once pulled a log train out of Deadwater that made a record trip down the mountain. By the time he'd cleared the first sharp reverse curve, Arthur realized the train was running too fast. He held back all he dared and whistled for the conductor to set his brake at the rear of the train. They were traveling at a good clip when the engine shot around the curve and out onto the band of steel over the Gulf. Behind the engine the logs and bunks were jumping and reeling; Arthur could feel their thundering momentum pushing at his back. Knocky Magoon, his young fireman, seemed to be enjoying their peril. He was watching backward over the swaying tender and laughing at the antics of the log bunks. Afterward, Arthur thought that there was something close to hysteria in Magoon's merriment. Bingham Heights station went by in a blur, Tupper holding the whistle wide open.

A new split switch had just been placed on the main line at Austin Junction. In theory, no matter how that switch was set, it should give a runaway train access to the rails heading south. Arthur prayed it would work. They hit the Junction, went through the switch, and headed toward Solon. The caboose had just cleared the road crossing below the Junction when a log bunk took off into the field, followed by its mates. No one on the rear end was hurt.

Log trains with ten loads were supposed to hold their speed to ten miles per hour. With more cars, the limit was set at six miles per hour. Some of the crews on the Somerset's log trains remembered runs where the speed was closer to sixty. Engine number 20 with ten loads got out of hand and went through to Solon before they got the train under control. Reed Hilton, who was on that run, remembered that it supplied enough excitement for a lifetime. You just hung on, wondering when a side rod would snap or a wheel leave the rail and bury you under a crisscross of logs and twisted metal. The danger of log trains reached beyond the mountain. The watchman's shanty at the Norridgewock highway crossing was once smashed when a chain broke on a load of logs. Fortunately, this happened in the middle of the night when the watchman was on duty.

Sometimes discretion was the better part of valor, and rear-end crews pulled the pin and didn't stay with a runaway train. Agent Woodard was down at Austin Junction one day waiting for a log train. The rumble of the train grew too rapidly. The engine appeared pitching down the last grade, followed by its careening train of logs. Woodard cleared the nearest snowbank in one jump, poking his head up in time to see the train disappear in a cloud of snow. There was no caboose. Some time later, as the agent was wading out of the snowbank, the lost caboose came rolling leisurely into the Junction with the conductor and the brakeman standing on the front platform, apparently enjoying the view.

The log bunks were a problem to the end. It took a special knack to handle a train of empty bunks. When the log-hauling era was over on the Somerset, the Maine Central sold the bunks to a New Hampshire concern, and a mainline engineer was sent to haul them down to Oakland. Agent Woodard warned him that empty bunks handled like snakes. Pulling into Embden to take water, the engineer made too strong an application on the engine brake, and the bunks went plunging over the fields around the station. They had to be retrieved one by one with a cable attached to the engine.

The progress in bringing the forests down was indicated by the laying of new and the abandoning of older sidings as logging operations were developed and completed. In 1911 the Somerset laid 1,549 feet of new turnouts. At the southern end of Moxie Pond, close to where Baker Stream enters, a spot called the Joe Hole became an important loading point. Long logs and pulp were brought down the lake like gigantic lily pads of wood encircled by a ring of boom logs. The boom was attached to a "headworks," a raft with a small, plank cabin and a large capstan. The capstan drum was the bottom section of a large log held vertically on a spindle supported overhead by a timber scaffold. Push bars fitted the mortises cut into the drum. A long hawser with an anchor attached to its free end was attached to the capstan. The anchor and rope were rowed out ahead of the headworks and dropped. Then the task began: Men bent over the push poles, walking the hours away around the capstan until the headworks and its small island of pulp or logs had come up to the anchor. With the anchor raised and set ahead, the warping would begin again.

Increasingly it was pulp that came ashore at the Joe Hole. A one-cylinder Root Van Root engine ca-chunked hour after hour driving the conveyor. Five rackcars a day were filled for the paper mill in Madison.

Forsythe, four-and-a-half miles north of Moxie Pond, was redolent with the smell of fresh-sawed pine and spruce. A short spur led between piles of lumber to the Skinner mill. This mill was sheathed in tar paper and wasn't much to look at, but its saws produced four million board feet per year. The Dutch oven under the mill's boiler burned the sawdust and slabs that made steam for the saws, for a donkey engine that hauled logs onto the conveyor, and for generating electricity. Any slabs left over were shipped to the paper mills at Madison. The mill ran day and night.

Walter Robinson, who operated several camps along the railroad, had the contract for cutting the logs. One of his larger operations was six miles up the tracks at Indian Pond, whose depot was another compact combination station with quarters for the agent and his wife attached to the rear. The long radio antenna rising from the roof of these quarters was a novel but essential feature—at least to the agent's wife who, understandably, didn't look forward to the long shut-in winter.

It took piles of supplies to keep an operation the size of Robinson's going, and they all had to be trundled from boxcars to the loading dock or manhandled directly to the waiting sleds. Stock for the camp's "wangan" ran to necessities: plug tobacco (B&L was the heavy favorite, but Spearhead and Battle Ax had their followings), wool socks, boot grease, and an assortment of liniments and

**The pickup flag is out at the little shelter in Forsythe. Woods operator
Walter Robinson (second from left); his clerk, Wiggy Small (center);
and others wait for the train.** AUTHOR'S COLLECTION

cure-alls. Allan Robinson–Walter's son–got a kick out of the wangan clerk.
Whenever a man came into the company store, the clerk would carefully fold his
newspaper just the way it had been thrown from the afternoon train, and wait on
the customer. Business over, the paper was unfolded again.

At train time men in heavy mackinaws and gum rubbers would collect on
the platform, talking and watching up the tracks. Occasionally you'd see a
woman barricaded behind suitcases or a brass-bound trunk. On winter mornings
a band of children in heavy knitted hats and boots waited for the train that took
them to school at Deadwater. The big crowds on the platform came in fall and
spring, when the crews assembled for the winter's hauling and the spring drive
down the river.

Across from the station was an old, well-established depot camp for the
Kennebec River drive. In spring Indian Pond Station became the supply base for
an army of rivermen. The gates of Indian Pond Dam were opened, and the drive
was on! A mile down the river was the "Hulling Machine," a bark-peeling stretch
of wild water that pounded with a terrific roar between the cliffs. Below this the
foaming river circled in Bow Hog Eddy–the place to look for the body of any

river driver who got sluiced down the falls above. Today the Hulling Machine has been flooded out by a hydro dam built just south of what was Indian Pond Station. Below this dam the Kennebec continues its descent and has become one of the best-known white-water rafting stretches in the country.

There was usually a need for men in the woods and always a flow of men coming and going. Over in Bangor the employment agency of Golden & Largie picked drifters off the street and shipped them back into the woods. During World War I the shortage of men became critical. Allan Robinson once went down to the depot to meet a car of recruits, only to find them dressed in low shoes and unable to tell which end of an ax handle should be hafted. After a dismal half-day trial, the railway hauled them back to the city.

Indian Pond was a busy place but not to be compared to Rockwood in fall, which was the staging base for a full-scale invasion. Forty cars a day of supplies and equipment were not unusual. Hand trucks rattled across the freight platform and thumped over the gangways to the waiting boats. Loaded cars were let down the slip track by cable until their floors were nearly awash and even with the decks of the scows.

The business of letting the boxcars down on a cable was a nuisance, and some crews wouldn't be bothered; they just bunted the cars down the ramp.

When it was time for the "down" train at Indian Pond, both loggers and school children collected on the station platform. AUTHOR'S COLLECTION

**A Baldwin engine built for the Seboomook Lake and St. John Railroad.
It was delivered in Rockwood but may not have traveled farther north.**
AUTHOR'S COLLECTION

Longtom Emery at the throttle overdid his push one day. George Giberson was riding the cartop and standing at the hand brake. He let out a bellow and jumped. The station agent had to borrow a tractor from the Great Northern to retrieve the car.

Moosehead was an inland waterway to the tote roads leading east and west from its shore–roads that ran up Tomhegan and Socatean Streams and west toward the Ross Farm and Lobster Lake. The Coburn steamboats were kept in constant operation hauling hay, beans, and other supplies from the railroad pier to the head of the lake–though some of the larger companies, such as American Realty, owned their own boats. Day and night, the preparations were made for another winter's attack on the spruce and pine.

North of Moosehead across the carry to the Penobscot waters, major operations were under way. The Great Northern was building a standard-gauge railroad from Seboomook to the headwaters of the St. John River. The Shay locomotive for this railroad arrived in Rockwood to be scowed up the big lake. This railroad was never completed; the engine along with a quantity of rail were eventually transported back to Rockwood and shipped out over the Somerset. Nevertheless, change had reached the North Woods–from ox to horse to steam to internal combustion engine almost in a single person's lifetime.

At the time of our story, though–the early 1900s–steam was still moving the wheels. A Maine man by the name of Alvin Orlando Lombard had found a way to take the locomotive off its rails and send it into the woods on steel treads. The Somerset hauled a number of these new steam log haulers north. The new

A steam-powered Lombard log hauler ready for a day's work at the Robinson operation in Deadwater. AUTHOR'S COLLECTION

job of "steerer" was created for only the brave at heart. Perched at the front of the hauler, numbed by cold and harassed by cinders, this fellow gripped his wheel and wrestled to keep the steering sled heading in the desired direction. On the level with a train of loaded sleds, a hauler could make four miles per hour. On a downhill run, speeds were to spoil the courage of many men. From Deadwater north, log haulers became part of the drama. They took water from the railway's tanks and contributed their columns of smoke and steam to the winter sky. Incidentally, these log haulers could be quite self-sufficient. A Ralph Ryder once delivered a Lombard into Buttermilk Pond; they cut wood for the firebox and, when needed, stopped at a brook and used the siphon hose to fill the tank.

In 1908 Hollingsworth & Whitney's began the largest of all the woods operations served by the Somerset. The railroad branch to the H&W's camps left the main line at Bald Mountain Station and swung generally east to the foot of Austin Pond. Here another branch followed the shoreline north, splitting into the "L-spur" to Bald Mountain Pond and another track to Little Austin Pond. It added up to twelve miles of trackage, all of which were in operation by 1913. The branch had its own water tank and a small wooden turntable used for turning snowplows. The Somerset engines backed into the branch to pick up their trains. The road had light ballast, and hauling was discontinued in spring. During the next nine years, the H&W cut four hundred thousand cords of pulp and shipped this wood to its paper mill in Madison.

Omar Sawyer was twenty-six when he became boss of the seven hundred men at work on the Bald Mountain cut. Omar had gone on his first drive when he was seventeen, and he had gone with a bad head cold. His mother was worried; there was still ice floating down the river. Riding a log downstream that first morning, Sawyer and a companion were swept under an overhanging tree, which brushed them into freezing water. According to Omar, the shock cured his cold. Sawyer was young, but he had learned how to handle troublemakers early on. When a big bruiser caused a scene in one of Sawyer's camps, Omar held him on the cookstove until the fellow pleaded. That had been in the old days. The job at Bald Mountain was like the managing of a big business—at least in some respects.

Sawyer and his wife moved into the boss's camp at the operation's home base. During one of Omar's frequent absences, Mrs. Sawyer made a frightful discovery. When her husband returned, she confronted him with the evidence. There, under the upturned tumble, was a bedbug. Omar went down to the big tin-sheathed warehouse that faced the tracks and got a wheelbarrow of sulfur. They plugged cracks in the walls and set the sulfur afire. After a time, looking in the camp windows, you could see nothing but a blue haze. The bedbugs either died or evacuated, but as long as the pair lived at Bald Mountain, Mrs. Sawyer could not keep her silver from turning black.

Life was never boring. The walking-boss knocked a young hawk off a post with a rock, and the Sawyers kept it as a pet. Omar's brother-in-law, Leon Bailey, was chief clerk; Mrs. Bailey and Mrs. Sawyer learned code from the station agent at Bald Mountain and kept in touch with all the news on the company telegraph line. There was excitement too, sometimes a lot more than anyone wanted.

The conveyor chain at number 15 clanked over the sprockets, and the pulp thudded into the rackcars. No one knows how the argument began. It was between two men, one standing on the staging above picking pulp off the conveyor, the other standing in the car below. The argument swiftly became a fight. As the fellow above started to slide down the sloping ramp, his adversary met him with a picaroon—a brutal instrument fit for the crusades, a double-bladed ax with the corners of its blades removed to form a sharpened point. It was over before anyone realized what was taking place. The picaroon sank deep into the pulp

A pulp-loading conveyor at Bald Mountain's camp No. 15, site of the "picaroon" murder. Six railroad cars could be loaded at once, and each was specially designed to offload more or less automatically at the paper mill in Madison.

picker's chest and pinned him to the ramp. The murderer tried to wrench the weapon free. Unable to do so, he fled. The conveyor crew tracked him down and turned him over to the sheriff, who arrived on the next freight train.

Ralph Barnie was an itinerant card shark and photographer who made the rounds of the Bald Mountain logging camps. His large bellowed camera took good pictures, and his fingers could make the cards dance. Barnie swore one day that he could transpose a deck of cards from the H&W office to the railroad station. When the agent got back to his station, there was the deck on his desk, right where Barnie had said it would be.

Leon Bailey needed a magician the day he forgot the combination on the safe. The Baileys had a private food cupboard in the root cellar behind the office camp. They kept the cupboard door locked, but someone sliced the leather hinges and raided their store. Later Leon saw one of his wife's preserve jars in the dump behind a camp occupied by some extra section hands. It wasn't a big theft–though his wife's preserves were special–but it got Leon to thinking. The payroll was twenty thousand dollars in cash; maybe, to be doubly safe, he ought to change the combination on the office safe now and then.

He wrote down the new combination on a slip of paper just until he was sure he had learned it. In the morning Leon met the train and took charge of the next shipment of money just as soon as the express man had opened the safe in the baggage car. But when he got back to the office camp, the combination he remembered would not work and the slip of paper could not be found. Leon kept the money under his mattress and sweated out the arrival of a locksmith from Bangor. The expert charged seventy-five dollars for opening the safe, and Leon, feeling the scrape was his fault, dug into his own savings to pay the bill.

For a time the Smitch Lumber Company, which specialized in broom handles, bought stumpage from the H&W. They laid side spurs of light track and experimented with using a Shay locomotive to twitch out big logs with a long cable. I've been told that you can still see the deep furrows plowed in the ground by the logs. The operation wasn't profitable. The company sold some of its equipment, including the twenty-thousand-gallon tank it had used to store fuel oil for its locomotive, to the H&W. The latter company made good use of the tank to store water for its tote-road icers, which sprayed the roads on winter nights and left ribbons of ice shining in the morning sun.

H&W tried its own innovation. Smitch's two old Pennsylvania Railroad coaches became sleeping quarters for the H&W portable sawmill, designed to cut trees into pulp. The mill with its saw was mounted on a flatcar and powered by a steam engine. The millcar was also equipped with a donkey engine and a cable to pull empty rackcars along a parallel siding for loading directly from the saw. The millcar was followed by a steam-generation plant–an old locomotive boiler mounted on a flatcar. Coal for the boiler's firebox was carried on the third car, and then came the two old coaches.

The mill sawed twelve thousand cords at Little Austin Pond before it was moved to other points along the branch. As the available timber moved farther from the tracks, the mill train became less effective. Finally, the boiler and engine were used to power the long conveyor at Camp Fifteen on Little Austin Pond. Pulp was sledded across the frozen pond. The teams and sleds were driven up onto a slating mound, and their loads spilled into the circle of water kept open with steam from the boiler. Pulp mounted the conveyor's ramp in a steady procession. It was carried along by an endless chain powered by an American Ball steam engine with a four-foot flywheel. The conveyor was a long trough elevated above the string of waiting rackcars. Every ten feet a section of trough could be dropped, allowing a man to hook the pulp sticks off the chain into the cars.

Bald Mountain runs were not prized by the railway men. Leon Greely, who lied about his age when he hired on as a brakeman, once left a crate of chickens sitting on a station platform, and they froze. The superintendent sent him to Bald Mountain until he had worked off the cost of the birds. He came close to freezing himself. There was one compensation: The railroad men could eat at the cook camp. The path through the snow to the camp was just wide enough for one foot in front of the other. Pat Hursey, possibly the heaviest engineer the Somerset ever had, could not manage the path, so he rolled to the feast.

And the forests came down. The Somerset had two very different faces: the smart countenance of the summer trade and the frostbitten grimace of the logging trains. One was pleasant, the other was the breadwinner. It was for the hauling of beans, hay, molasses, oats, and townships of timber that the Somerset's extension had been built. The rest was white sunshades and gravy.

Chapter Ten

THE WILD COUNTRY

Aʙᴏᴠᴇ Bɪɴɢʜᴀᴍ, the Somerset left behind the villages of trim white houses, the churches, shops, and doctors' offices. What the track now ran through was not wilderness so much as it was frontier. It was a country with a wild streak.

After a winter in the logging camps, many men came out to the Somerset's rails with a howl of conquest. It was time to blow their dam and let out a flood of emotions. Of course, a good many loggers were housebroken. They worked in

River drivers, a vanished breed of men. AUTHOR'S COLLECTION

the woods all winter, drove the season's cut on the spring freshets, collected their wages, and went home to their wives and their farms. Still, the roaring tradition of the "Bangor men"—a term indicating a temperament rather than a residence—was authentic enough.

There were times when conductors deserved hazardous-duty pay. A coach full of loggers just out of camp and heading for town could be trouble. When men started rolling down the aisles like logs in white water, the conductor found another use for his lamp stick. This stick had a wick on one end for lighting the hanging lamps and a hook on the other for opening the windows in a coach's clerestory. Between the wick and the hook was a solid piece of oak with which a man could clear a considerable swath.

The bigger towns were favorites of loggers looking to spend their wages in a few weeks, but Somerset Junction was closer. Whiskey and rum could be bought by the dipperful, women were available, and a good fight was free. From the first, Somerset Junction was a rough place. Before the tracks had even been spiked down, five hundred dollars had been stolen from the paymaster's camp. The telegraph line had been cut, and the trail was cold by the time the sheriff arrived.

Somerset Junction, looking west down the Canadian Pacific's main line. The three-storied white building to the right is the Somerset House.
AUTHOR'S COLLECTION

To provide facilities for the lumbermen and loggers, Henry Bartley built a hotel at the Junction. Strangely, it was built of southern pine, but no one objected. The saloon in the basement fitted in perfectly and was soon the busiest place around. Tobacco smoke braided around the hanging lamps; there was the ruffle of cards and constant clink of tin dippers. When things became too riotous, Henry cleared the men out and locked the door.

But the malignant effects of alcohol lurked in the dark corners of this rough-and-tumble world. One fellow, finding himself locked out of the saloon, clawed at the door bellowing like a bear. Finding the panels too tough for his fingernails, he grabbed an ax and began swinging. Inside the saloon someone got nervous and pulled the trigger on the shotgun kept under the bar. The buckshot splintered through the door, hitting the drunken man in the stomach. He died soon after they got him to Greenville.

At Christmas the saloon was decorated with evergreen trees set all around the walls. The aroma of the young spruce made the loggers feel at home. These decorations were largely responsible for the hotel's fiery end, and it was Doc Prithim's cold hands that may have saved the sleeping boarders in the hotel.

Doctor Fred Prithim was an outstanding physician who served Greenville and much of the area around. He snowshoed miles to deliver babies and waded flooded trails to perform emergency operations in a woods camp. When possible, Doc traveled on horseback, catching a little sleep while his Kentucky mare took him home.

The night in question was a cold one, cold even for December. Stars arched above, many bright enough to have been the Magi's guide. Doc Prithim followed the Somerset track. The new baby he'd just delivered in Rockwood had refused to be hurried, and Doc had missed the last train. Usually he carried his equipment in a wicker pack especially made for the purpose by a local Indian, but this night he was toting his buggy satchel and a bag of obstetric tools. His hands, despite the two pairs of mittens, were getting stiff.

At Somerset Junction the doctor stopped in at the Bartley House to warm his hands and feet and get some rope. He wanted to tie his bags together to carry them around his neck. The night clerk was dead asleep; only after a series of yawns did he shuffle out to the kitchen and return with some twine. Doc tied the bags together and set out on the last twelve miles of his hike to Greenville.

His nap already interrupted, the night clerk decided he might as well check the big heater in the saloon. When he opened the door to the cellar, flames shot up the stairs. His frantic calls awoke those sleeping in the rooms above. The station agent and his new bride jumped from a second-story window, leaving their wedding presents behind.

Down the Canadian Pacific track, meantime, Doc Prithim trudged along more asleep than awake. His first thought was that the moon was rising behind him and casting its red glow on the snow. Then it came to him that the moon does not rise in the west. He turned. The Bartley House was having its last red-hot time.

Martin Munster built the next hotel at the Junction and called it, in a burst of originality, the Somerset House. Some people got confused and referred to it as the "Monster House," but Martin and his wife Mary ran a much better-than-average logger's haven. Still, Doc Prithim never sat down to eat at the Somerset House. He figured that some of the waitresses might have too many occupations. He would go out into the kitchen, cut slices of meat and bread, and brown them himself on the hot stove.

Railroad crews lived in a bunkcar at the Junction and minded their own business. It was not healthy to tangle with the logging crews. Lumberjacks might stamp on each other's chests and tattoo one another with their teeth, but if it came to a general fight, they would band into an army. A wise man went to the hotel saloon in the company of his buddies and preferably with the biggest brakeman he could find. Some of the Somerset boys went so far as to carry brake sticks tucked up their sleeves. You learned to look behind you and to stay with your friends.

Even in the bunkcar a man wasn't completely safe. One fellow had just returned from the Somerset House and was pulling off his socks when a knock came at the door, and someone called out his name. Stepping out, he was met with a lantern held close to his face. Then the lantern was jerked back and swung with full force. The trainman ended up with a broken nose and a cut across his left cheek. No one in the crew ever found out what the altercation was about.

The real danger, however, was not from the loggers, rough as they could be. The dealers in violence and the bushwhackers belonged to the fringe, the stealthy creepers in the shadows–the twisted ones. Doc Prithim often had men follow him on his nightly trips. Evidently these stalkers thought that a physician would be carrying money, and Doc made sure that no one got a chance to jump him.

The outstanding female character at the Junction was called "Blueberry," which alluded to an extended vein in her forehead. One Somerset man observed that when sober, Blueberry weighed two hundred pounds; drunk, she weighed closer to three hundred, most of which was muscle. But it was not only her weight that commanded respect. She kept a big butcher knife under the counter in her boardinghouse, and no one was allowed to forget that it was there.

Blueberry ran her own bootlegging business. If competition was tremendous, opportunity was greater. While the revenue officers knew many of the routes over the border, the smugglers knew more. It was like trying to plug a fishnet with a limited supply of cork stoppers.

Typically, Blueberry took the bold approach, which cut out any middleman. Her runner worked directly with the Canadian contacts and used a pumpcar on the Canadian Pacific tracks. One night the runner failed to return. His pumpcar was eventually found, but there was no other trace. The joke around the bunkcar was that he had been spirited away.

The wave of logging moved northward, taking with it much of Somerset Junction's transient population. Still, the Junction's reputation persisted. Logger Burke Connoughton, dog-tired from trying to beat the set-in of mud season, stopped at the Junction to get a meal. He ate and fell asleep with his head and arms resting on the table. He awoke feeling that his nap had done him no good. Then he realized that he was in the midst of a broken chair.

The hotel at Rockwood had been built by Governor William Haines and was owned and run by the Somerset Railway. The loggers were segregated to the annex. One railroader remembered that fare was pretty good, and some of the "boys" found plenty to drink–Pink Rose Whisky (nicknamed "joy-water"), Carmalion Whisky ("stagger juice"), and the bootlegged stuff (aptly called "boiler wash"). There was moose meat and venison in season. Out of season there was mutton and veal, which often tasted like moose and deer meat.

Water was only in short supply once, when the fifty-thousand-gallon standpipe that rose behind the hotel was mysteriously drained. Suspicions fell on Old Jack, an Indian who had just been fired. Old Jack probably held no animosity. He had been getting two dollars a cord for firewood cut, split, and piled in the woodshed. There were plenty of other fellows around Rockwood, however, who would pull such a stunt just to pass the time.

Among the railroaders, the younger men found places to go when things got dull around Rockwood, such as the dance hall up at Moose River. It was well worth walking the "carry," a woods trail from Rockwood to Moose River, to dance with one of the dark-eyed Sockabasin girls. They stayed with the man who'd brought them to the dance and never made any comments about their partner's awkwardness.

It was more expensive to go to a dance held for the help at Kineo House across the lake. A ride on the boat cost a dollar for a round trip. No one was allowed into the dance if his breath smelled of alcohol. Once inside, though, the predominance of females was intoxicating enough.

Getting back to Rockwood could be an adventure. Crossing the "Big Lake" could be tricky, especially in the fog. Reed Hilton and some buddies got in on such an adventure one night. As the boat started back to Rockwood, a blanket of fog quickly hid Kineo House's many lights. That was their last bearing until the boat struck and slid up on a mudbank somewhere along the shore of the Moose River. No one was more surprised than the skipper. After knocking down every passenger standing on the deck, the boat slipped back into the water. Some hours later, the skipper managed to find Rockwood and tie up to the railroad pier.

While the telegraph remained the official language of the railway, the telephone line was important. Hung lower on the poles than the telegraph wires, the phone lines often survived the sleet storms that played havoc with conventional communications. The phone was useful for section crews and indispensable for railroad wives isolated in section houses and at stations along the track from Bingham to Kineo.

But up in the wild country, the telephone could get you into a mess. The station agent's wife at Moxie called her grocery order down to Bingham one day; it included a two-pound roast, a pound of rock salt, and a gallon of molasses. When the wayfreight pulled into Moxie there was a side of beef, fifty pounds of rock salt, and thirty gallons of molasses. The sun was hot, and so was the train crew when they loaded the stuff back into the boxcar. The meat was ripening from its travel.

People along the line kept in touch through the phone—too closely for one agent's welfare. While his wife was away, he invited his "cousin" to come for the week. The agent's wife had observant friends, however, who called her and described some items of clothing that the "cousin" had hung on the line behind the station. The wife called her husband, and the "cousin" answered. The next train brought the wife—a formidable woman when she was mad. She was preceded by a call from a friend of the agent, who feared for his safety. He should have left with the "cousin." It may not be true, as reported by the crew of number 7, that they had almost run into her pumping north on a three-wheeler. It was certain, however, that the agent next appeared behind his ticket window with a black eye and swollen left ear.

The phone might have prevented a really tragic episode up at Moxie, but it didn't. A husband returned home unexpectedly to find his wife had taken in another man. Rifle in hand, he burst through the door, shooting and wounding his wife. The man jumped through a window. He made several circuits of the

The railroad station at Lake Moxie in 1925.

cabin with the husband at his heels, firing all the time. Seeing no future in this ring around the rosy, the fellow made a desperate sprint up the tracks. The station agent said he seemed to be staying ahead of the bullets. The down passenger train pulled in shortly after the husband had fired his last round. The wounded wife was loaded into the baggage car. She lived.

The phone connected the people along the Somerset rails north of Bingham with the doctor. Called in an emergency, doctors were often taken north on the lineman's motorcar. After several incidents of leaving the iron and landing in the bushes, there were complaints that the linemen took such errands of mercy as an excuse for traveling too fast. Still, it took a lot to discourage those small-town medical men. If a call came in from a woods camp or from one of the little settlements along the rails, Dr. Percivel Hopkins of Bingham would pull his hat brim down tightly and tuck his bag under the seat of the motorcar.

The telephone wire was but a thin strand threading through the wild country. In real ways, isolation remained. If a man had sliced his foot with an ax and was bleeding to death, the emergency was immediate. Folks had to call upon the older ways. A good blood charmer—there were some about—had to be careful not to stop the flow so quickly that blood poisoning set in. Down in the villages

133

along the Kennebec, charming, cures, omens, and a sense of unseen powers were becoming submerged—an underground stream—but in the wild country this occult stream bubbled up to the surface. It flowed through daily life because it was needed and because it seemed at home in the dark shadows of the woods.

The young station agent at Bald Mountain Station, like an Ichabod Crane, listened with rapt attention to the stories told in the Hollingsworth & Whitney camps—stories of the "dingmale," a creature heard but never seen; of the devil dancing on a camp roof in Enchanted Township; of phantom figures walking the tote roads; of snarled chains that foretold of death, and ghost lights that haunted the night. The more he heard, the less he liked walking down to Dimmick Siding at night to see a girl who lived there. The clerk at the H&W's depot camp once hung a lantern in a fir tree by the path, just to give the young agent a start. It did, but the strange thing was that when the clerk went to retrieve the lantern that next morning, he found it still burning with a full reservoir of oil. As near as the clerk could see, there were only his own tracks in the snow around the tree.

Strange things happened north of civilization. Bakers was a flag stop just south of milepost 57 that boasted two identical houses built for section crew families. Each home had its own outhouse, and behind these little buildings Baker Stream flowed between banks of alders. It was just south of this flag stop that the engineer of the night Pullman spotted what appeared to be a red lantern. He stopped, and the brakeman went forward to investigate. There was neither lantern nor anything unusual to be found. The train arrived late at Oakland for its connection with the Maine Central's Bar Harbor train. The dispatcher suspected that the crew had just made up an excuse.

It soon became apparent that this was not the case. Two more trains were stopped by the "ghost light" at Bakers. John Vigue was at the throttle of the fourth train to see the red lantern, with Reed Hilton firing. They had just rounded the curve and passed the section houses at Bakers when John slammed in the throttle. He motioned to Reed to come over to his side. Together they peered out the window at the track ahead. The yellow glare of the headlight made a tunnel through the blackness—and ahead was a reddish something glowing beside the track. Reed, the front-end brakeman, and the baggage master all went forward. It seemed like a three-man expedition.

The light disappeared and they found nothing to explain what they had seen. No one ever did. The order was sent out from the office to pay no more attention to red signals just below Bakers. The light was reported several more times, and then it was seen no more. Some people suggested that the light had been fox fire; other guessed that someone had simply grown tired of seeing trains pass Bakers without stopping. No one knew the cause, but people remembered the "warning light" later when one of the few passenger train wrecks occurred just where that light had been seen. It was a serious derailment that left the passengers shaken, though no one was killed.

Alas, investigation explained too many of the mysteries along the railway. When his train stopped at Moxie, newly promoted Conductor Leon Greely walked its length, checking the journals and brakes. Reaching the baggage car, he set his lantern on the cinders and bent over to tie his shoe. As he straightened up there came a strange noise. It sounded like someone playing on a loose string of a bass viol. Then it came again, and from inside the car. The baggage master was nowhere to be seen, and Greely was sure someone was tampering with the baggage. Grabbing his lantern, he climbed into the car and, holding his light over his head, peered into the dark corners. No one; yet the noise continued. It seemed to be coming from a large milk can. Taking off the lid, Greely tipped his lantern to look inside. The largest frogs he had ever seen stared back at him. They and their legs were on the way to the big hotel at Kineo.

While you might doubt manifestations of the supernatural, there was no question about the powers of the storms that swept the wild country. One spring brought a freshet that flooded the track at Deadwater. The Hollingsworth & Whitney Company was anxious to get a train of pulp through, and Engineer Charlie Ireland volunteered. The water was up to the grates, and there was no way to tell what lay ahead or under them. Halfway through the flooded area a loose rail shot up between the engine's drivers like a steel serpent, smashed through the storm window, just missed Charlie's head, and rammed out the rear of the cab. Ireland turned and grinned at his fireman. "You can't kill an Irishman," he said. That wasn't true. Ireland was to lose his life some years later "working out" an engine just refurbished in the shops.

Even genteel summer brought its tempests–storms when the lightning would produce an eerie corona (St. Elmo's fire) around the handle of the air brake in a locomotive cab. One night such a storm developed over the mountains and, having felt its strength by playing havoc with the fir trees, swept down on the Somerset. Train number 118 rounded a curve going forty (fast for the Somerset) and met a large oak blown down across the track. The stack was bent sideways, the whistle and bell stripped off, and all the glass shattered on the engineer's side. They made Bingham two hours late.

And winter! Winter deserves and will get its own chapter.

It was frontier country, wild and beautiful. Moxie Mountain ruled the valley of the Austin. Where the railway entered the folding hills above Bingham, you could see glimpses of Moxie rising blue-green and shouldering the sky. It was as if the Somerset's sole destination was this mountain. As the locomotive rounded the curve above the Austin bridge, there was Moxie, scored and scarred by time, ice, and rock slides but filling the north with its magnificence. At Dimmick Siding you saw Moxie's eastern flank, while ahead new mountains swept townships of forest upward to white crowns of cumulus. To the east stretched the bare back of Bald Mountain darkening the water of Moxie Pond. Farther north rose Squaw Mountain, and finally the inland sea of Moosehead and the wall of Kineo.

Like all frontiers, the wild country didn't last very long. Expanding populations may finally bring their own sophisticated "wilderness" to this cut-over land. Whatever happens, it will be well to remember that here once trod a breed of loggers who could spit across Baker Stream, a race of women who could make the woods bow down and murmur "home," and crews of railroad men who dared to bring the log trains down from Deadwater.

Chapter Eleven

TWENTY BELOW AND BLOWING

WITH A SEEMING RELUCTANCE, the sun lifted itself above the hill. It was red, but as the Good Book says of David in his old age, "It gat no heat." By noon it was a dull white disk nearly obscured in the graying sky. The wind had backed into the northeast, and all the signs said "blizzard" except perhaps the temperature. It felt too cold to snow. But the snow was coming. By early afternoon the agent at Rockwood telegraphed that the storm was sweeping across the frozen expanse of lake and hiding the wall of Mount Kineo.

It was an old scenario and another headache for Forrest Fowels, the Somerset's dispatcher. Lester Williams had dropped by the office, and together they had reminisced on storms that had buried the railway. Fowels got to talking about the new plows and what a difference they made, and Williams, with the way he had of telling stories, recalled an incident when he was station agent up in North Anson.

As Lester remembered, it was back in March 1907 that he'd received orders for the plow train working south (that would be west in railroad parlance) out of Bingham, and he'd hung out the red lantern. That done, he was standing at the bay window watching the dance of flakes around the ruby light when, in a tornado of flying snow, something large and dark swept past. The swirling snow settled; the track was empty. Lester was out on the platform trying to figure out what had gone by when the plow train came drifting into North Anson Yard. The locomotive worked steam past the freight shed and rolled to a stop before the station.

"You seen our plow?" the engineer yelled down to Lester. "The damned thing broke loose when I set the brake above town."

By then Lester was aware of the ten-by-ten timber attached to the engine's front coupling and slanting down into the sifting snow between the rails.

"You know what you've been pushing for the last half mile?" he called back.

"Good God, it's the plow's center sill," the engineer said in a half whisper when he joined Lester, and he turned as white as the blowing snow.

"You remember that spring blizzard, Forrest?" Lester asked now.

Fowels nodded. He remembered the "storm of 1907"—even the smallest details. He remembered the morning of the storm's height. He had set his coffee mug on yesterday's paper, right on a quarter-page ad for Hall's Sarsaparilla. It had seemed premature to be promoting a cure for the spring humors. It certainly hadn't been spring on that March morning. During the night a blizzard had invaded the Kennebec Valley. He had sat in this same chair and listened to the staccato reports from stations along the Somerset's ninety miles. One after the other they were being snowed in.

There had been a major tie-up at Bingham. Fowels had raised Pearl Woodard, the Bingham agent, before it was light—the telegraph had by then been installed by the station master's bed. Fowels needed a plow train made up to

Cold weather at Bingham's passenger station. The Bingham Hotel's winter hack—a horse-drawn sleigh—is on the left. AUTHOR'S COLLECTION

clear the line to Oakland. Later, Woodard told Fowels how that snow-filled morning had gone.

Pearl had put on his long, winter coat, pulled on his boots, and wallowed from house to boardinghouse calling the crew. His lantern had made little light in the tempest. By half past six the waiting room in Bingham had warmed appreciably. The plow train had disappeared into the gray sweep of snow south of the water tank. Despite the weather, Woodard had sold several tickets by the time the passenger train had been made up. While Conductor Cote joined the group around the stove, Pearl shoveled a path across the platform to the waiting coach. Behind him, the wind kept busy scooping out a hollow around that corner of the station and piling a sharp-edged drift across the newly cleared planks. The snow was that heavy, granular stuff made for packing into dense drifts. The rate it was accumulating surprised the agent.

At seven A.M. train number 12 left with a baggage car, one coach, half a dozen passengers, and the mail. Woodard had sent a report to Fowels and was dumping more coal into the stove when Cote appeared to announce that his train was stuck.

There were two engines still in the roundhouse, one a new Baldwin ten-wheeler. Pearl sent her down to rescue the stranded train. It was a stirring sight. The locomotive had her cylinder cocks open like the nostrils of a dragon spewing steam, but the ten-wheeler ended up getting stuck as well. The half-dozen passengers returned to the waiting room stove while Woodard called for reinforcements from the section crew.

Shoveling was next to useless, though they tried. The drifting was fierce. The stuck passenger coach was buried up to the coach windowsills by this time. Something had to be done, and sending down the remaining engine seemed fruitless. Woodard returned to the station. He telegraphed the dispatcher to hold the eastbound train at Solon—if it had managed to get that far.

The buildings broke the wind in the upper part of the yard, and less drifting was taking place; it occurred to Pearl that the remaining engine might push a string of empty rackcars down to the stuck engine and train and, with enough shoveling and sanding of rail, haul them back. It worked. At one o'clock that afternoon, the early-morning passenger train left Bingham, preceded by another plow train. This plow train had orders to run to North Anson, turn, and then precede the eastbound waiting at Solon.

Pearl had snowshoed down to Austin Junction, and he got on the locomotive of the passenger train when it arrived. "Give her all she got," he had told the engineer. Halfway into Bingham, the engineer had caught sight of the plow train ahead through a momentary lull in the blowing snow and instinctively shoved in the throttle. Woodard had come off the fireman's box where he had been riding and yelled at the engineer to keep the engine going. They had managed to pull in. It had been a long day already.

All this time Fowels had been having his own problems. By five o'clock that evening a group of passengers had gathered at the Oakland depot, clamorous for one more train north. The superintendent had yielded, and Fowels made up a train with one coach, two engines, and a plow. He issued orders to break out the line as far as Madison. The expedition got no more than a mile out of Oakland. Fowels sent two more engines–which, having joined the stranded train, got stuck and were soon drifted in. The passengers had to be brought back to Oakland and put up in a hotel, where they had stayed for the next two days. Oakland Yard had become a drifted desert of snow, and the volunteer fire department was called to fill the tanks of stranded Somerset and Maine Central locomotives. Shovels were the only weapon against drifts built by such a storm. When the weather cleared, the Somerset had hired every man and good-sized boy it could find and paid them ten cents an hour to clear tracks and switches in the railroad yard.

Sleds of hay begin the long haul to woods camps. Rockwood Hotel is in the immediate background. GAIL TURMEL COLLECTION

"I hope I am retired before we have another blizzard like that," Fowels told Lester Williams now as Lester was leaving.

When Fowels reviewed the present situation, things looked pretty good. The log trains were in from Deadwater, the passenger runs were pretty much on schedule, and freight number 37, though late, would soon be in Rockwood. It was snowing hard as far south as Madison, but the railway's heaviest equipment was strategically positioned at Bingham and Rockwood, ready to plow out the line.

At dusk the snow reached Oakland with the wind full at its back. Shortly after seven, Wyman, the night operator, got a call for help. Just south of Rockwood the locomotive on train 37 had hit an ice-blocked switch point. All her drivers had left the rails. Fifty tons of motive power had become helpless in less than ten seconds.

Reed Hilton had enjoyed a dinner with his parents and girlfriend, and he was helping with the supper dishes when Wyman called. With the snow and wind blowing outside, the whole family had settled down in the kitchen. His father disliked telephones and had sworn that he would rip the thing off the wall someday. Reed wished he had.

Hay load preceded by a snowplow drawn by a double team. Shown in front of the railroad's Rockwood Store. GAIL TURMEL COLLECTION

Reed's job was to round up the crew for the wreck train. John Vigue, the engineer, said a great deal in French when Reed called him. Fireman Ernest Priest's English was equally forceful. Assistant Superintendent George Foster met them at the yard, and they assembled the usual cars–a platform car, two toolcars, one cookcar, and a caboose. When they backed down to the station, Foster ordered a wedge plow and a flanger put on behind the caboose.

As long as an engine could wade through the snow, the Somerset pulled its wedge plows; it was a lot safer that way. Home-built of hard pine, the wedges were mounted on two single trucks and ballasted with sand. Most of this weight ended up over the plow's rear wheels, accentuating the wedge's propensity for rearing up and smashing itself or something else. There was no provision for a man to ride these plows. No one was that foolish anyway.

The shop built the flangers as well, starting with a beefed-up boxcar with a "digger" blade slung underneath for clearing the snow from between the rails. This blade had to be raised to clear switches and road crossings, an operation accomplished with a hand crank mounted inside the car. The crank operator worked blindly, depending on orders to raise and lower the blade from his companion stationed at a small, boxlike window protruding from the side of the car. Reed pulled the job of lookout and Charles Lord, the track foreman, took the hand crank.

The train made good time for the first twenty miles, but the accumulation of snow increased as they went north. The flanger was smothered in a white cloud, and Reed was having trouble keeping the side window clear. They rumbled through the covered bridge and passed the North Anson Station. Just north of the village cemetery, the digger blade caught a raised plank in the road crossing. The blade twisted under the flanger's rear wheels. In a jolting few seconds the car lurched, parted with the plow and the rest of the train, and went over on its side. The little potbellied stove went over, its coals rattling against the wall that had suddenly become the floor.

Reed and Charles managed to keep the car from igniting. Reed stood on the cranking frame and forced open the side door, which was now overhead. The train had disappeared northward into the storm, evidently unaware of any loss. To make matters worse, Charles told Reed that he thought he had broken his wrist.

There was a section carhouse a few rods down the track, and the two men walked to its shelter. Reed lit a lamp, stirred up the fire left by the section crew, and fashioned a makeshift sling for his buddy's arm. They sat down close to the stove and waited while the wind whistled in the cracks. Half an hour later the

Deadwater Station in the grips of a Maine winter. AUTHOR'S COLLECTION

train reappeared, backing slowly with the conductor standing spread-legged on the rear of the plow, his lantern held high.

Charles went to the caboose and Reed climbed into the engine cab. Ahead, the world narrowed to a tunnel of light moving through the blizzard.

At Bingham, halfway to the derailed engine, Charles was sent to the doctor. Vigue had no notion how long they would be out and wanted to be sure they had plenty of coal. The engine was uncoupled and run down to the coaling yard. Ordinarily, a locomotive would be attached to the crane cable. It then ran a short distance ahead, hoisting the huge tubs up to its own tender. But on this night the rails were iced, and the drivers spun. There was a hand windlass for such situations. Reed took his turn at the crank. It was twenty below, and the grease peeled from the gears hard and brittle.

They headed up the grade to Deadwater. Reed spelled Priest bailing coal into the orange swirl of the firebox. He braced his butt against the rounded projection of the tender and began the never-ending task. The engineer had no choice but to give the locomotive all the head she had. When the drivers slipped, Vigue would ease off and lay sand, but the surging exhaust caused by the thrashing wheels tore the fire apart, which added to the fireman's problems. At Deadwater the spout on the water tank was frozen solid and had to be thawed with a torch of improvised rags soaked in oil before it could be lowered. While Priest put water in the tender, Reed worked over the fire getting rid of the largest

A late-winter view of Rockwood and the railroad yard.
On the left, a wooden, horse-drawn road plow awaits the next storm.
AUTHOR'S COLLECTION

clinkers. Vigue waded around his engine with a lantern inspecting what he could see, but snow was packed in up to the running boards.

Over the grade, the train picked up some speed. Since Bingham they had been pushing one of the new Roger wing plows, which was tossing great white plumes right and left; now the flying snow blew in around the cab's curtains, turning to slush on the back of the fireman. Unless he was ambidextrous and could fire either right or left, a man wet-froze on one side and got fire-roasted on the other. Along the shores of Moxie Pond, it was blowing a gale; the cab filled with melting flakes. Reed got wet on both sides. When his time-out came, he got as close to the boiler back-head as he could to keep from freezing.

There was an early-morning grayness in the flying snow when they reached the stranded train. It had stopped snowing, but it was still blowing and twenty below. They pulled the freight cars back to Somerset Junction so that they could get at the derailed locomotive. Foster sent Vigue, Reed, and Priest back to the cookcar to get some dry clothes and grub. He wanted Vigue rested and the other two men ready to help get the locomotive back on the iron.

144

The tender came back onto the rails without much complaint, but the engine was a far larger problem. It took a hour of shoveling, crawling around in the drifts, rigging blocks, hauling bull chains, and setting rerails before the front pilot wheels were back on the rails. Then there was another two hours of freezing work—jacking and the laying of temporary rail—before they were ready for the final pulls. Vigue was back in the rescue engine's cab, hopefully rested and wide awake. The section crew from Rockwood had shoveled the rails clear under his locomotive and covered them with sand. Vigue eased the engine back. The cables came taut. It was the engineer's skill that was being tested now. The pull had to be slow and smooth. The drivers came up on the temporary rail. Vigue eased off and the tackle was changed for the sideways slip, which would put the locomotive back on the main line again.

It was midmorning before the task was done. When they pulled into Rockwood, the sky was a startling blue between the shreds of clouds sweeping eastward. Rockwood Yard was a sea of moving snow fleeing before the strong, clearing wind. The Oakland men had hoped they could lay over in Rockwood to thaw out and rest, but their new orders were to return to Oakland as a plow train clearing the main line and sidings to Bingham.

Spurgeon Hoar, the mechanical foreman, came along just as Reed was climbing on the caboose. "My wife was reading someplace," Spurgeon said, "that the bottom of hell is all frozen over. I suppose that some people would find that strange."

"I suppose," Reed responded.

Forrest Fowels remembered when it snowed sometime during the day for thirty consecutive days up at Somerset Junction. Knowing that the Junction was located in a place called Misery Gore should have prepared him for such conditions; still, it must have been a long winter. The Somerset bunted, plowed, and shoveled its way through these "old-fashioned winters." To those living in such isolated northern settlements, the plow train's whistle must have brought a sense of liberation. Lumber outfits found their hay bales stacked in a drift where a buried tote road met a siding, housewives got the Wards catalog, and old men received their evening papers.

And the winter of the Christmas card also existed. There was splendor in the pristine, crystal world of winter. One railroader who, in his old age, moved to where there was no real winter told me of a dream that came to him when nights were hot and stuffy. He was back in an engine easing into Solon. In the beam of the headlight the snowflakes drifted, and there was no sound except the rhythmic music of the side rods. The station lights were a warm yellow in the blue and

145

purple world of a soft winter evening. A blanketed horse with a sleigh was waiting beside the snow-frosted canopy, and it seemed there was no hurry anymore.

Looking back, Reed Hilton remembered:

"I rather enjoyed seeing the snow take a beating, especially if it were a big drift or a snow slide which took to the air. It was exciting when seen from the monkey cage of a plow at forty-five miles per hour.

"Snow seemed whiter above Bingham, and as cold as it would be, it was pretty. . . . I get to thinking now and then what a thrill I used to get riding the head end or the hack lookout on a moonlight night. You saw the country as God made it."

Chapter Twelve

WHITE SUNSHADES

How beautiful the morning breaks
Upon the king of mountain lakes;
The forest, far as the eye can search,
Stretches green and still from either beach,
And leagues away the waters gleam
Resplendent in the sunrise beam;
Yet feathery vapors, circling slow,
Wreath the dark brow of Kineo.

— FRANCES MACE

IN 1882 LUCIUS HUBBARD published *Hubbard's Guide to Moosehead Lake and Northern Maine.* Primarily for the "canoe-man," the little manual instructed the adventurer where to go and how to camp. In a pocket attached to the back cover was Hubbard's map, thought by many old-time guides to be the best on the market. Hubbard's introduction discloses the appeal of the life closer to nature that was increasingly luring people to the Maine woods: "To the care worn business man and overwhelmed student, no relaxation from the constant wear of their respective calling is so grateful as that which comes while camping in the woods." Hubbard quotes from a Reverend Julius Ward, who had written in *Harpers* magazine: "The accompaniments of life are removed and selfish ambition and care have no place [in the woods], a man is most truly thrown on his own resources."

Thoreau, first in letters and thoughts among the Maine woods travelers, would have agreed in principle. And Theodore Roosevelt, with his rod and gun and his love for wilderness areas like the Moosehead, would have said, "Bully."

Subtract the blackflies and it was (and is) an unbeatable experience. Salt pork sizzling in the pan, trout waiting to be fried, the dark river quietly passing beneath the overhanging boughs, a moose wading in the shallows, and above, the timbered mountains set in amber by the setting sun.

What began as a catering service for a relatively few seeking adventure in the wilderness became the business of supplying rustic comfort to a growing multitude of summer vacationers and sportsmen–and sportswomen, too, if the brochure photos of ladies in jodhpurs holding strings of fish or standing beside a strung-up deer are reliable.

Maine was becoming "vacationland." In keeping with this new image, the state's display at the 1904 St. Louis Exposition was a two-story log lodge complete with a large stone fireplace, an open loft, and lots of deer heads. Two years later the Somerset Railway, newly arrived at Moosehead, announced its intention to enter the vacationing business by publishing the *Sportsman's Map of the Upper Kennebec and Moosehead Regions*.

The map was not in the same league with the Bangor & Aroostook's yearly publication, *The Maine Woods*. Amounting to a small book, *The Maine Woods* was a top-of-the-line publication advertising as a sportsman's paradise the huge area served by the B&A. Still, the Somerset was in an enviable position. Its Rockwood railhead was surrounded by sporting camps and directly across from one of New England's grand hotels. It was also twenty miles nearer the head of the lake and canoe trips into that vast land of rivers and lakes. The Somerset was, as it advertised, the Kineo Short Line.

Another book for adventurers in Maine was Captain Farrar's *Illustrated Guide Book to Moosehead*. When it was written, the Somerset had just reached Solon. Farrar described the considerable journey from this new railhead to the big lake. From Solon you took a stage to Bingham, thence up the Kennebec to Caratunk, and then to the Forks. The total time for this journey, including stops, was about ten hours. That enterprising entrepreneur of the upper Kennebec, Abner Coburn, had built a hotel at the Forks that could take a hundred guests. Water was "carried" to all three floors, and there was a piano. Farrar indicates that from the Forks there was a road of sorts through Moxie and Indian Pond to Moosehead; it must have been a rough buckboard journey.

Seventeen years later it took only sixteen and a half hours to ride from New York to Kineo, and a good deal of that was spent in a Pullman bed. Compared to stage travel, prices were down as well. It cost 75 cents to travel by stage from Solon to Bingham, a distance of eight miles, while you paid $14.80 for a round-trip ticket from Boston to Kineo.

There were plenty of trout in the north country in those days. These men, with the exception of the third from the right, were guides for the Kineo Hotel in Rockwood. MOOSEHEAD HISTORICAL SOCIETY

With this increased accessibility, people came in great numbers to vacation at the sporting camps north of Deadwater. Mike Marr's camps on Indian Pond had their own station. It was a small, neat building with a combination baggage-waiting room and a wide overhang on one gable end that served as additional shelter. There was no record that this station ever had an agent, but it was a regular stop, which indicates the importance that the "vacation/sporting industry" had assumed. The proprietors assured those who came to stay at their camps that they would be happy. In the words of their ad, there was "plenty of room to live in." Food was good, with fresh vegetables grown in the camp's garden. For those who wanted to leave the comforts of the main lodge and go farther afield, guides and canoes were ready, and there were outlying camps at Indian and Chase Streams.

This attractive little building served as a shelter for passengers and baggage coming and going between the Somerset's flag stop and Marr's Camps.

The rustic beauty of Marr's Camps on Indian Pond, far from the madding crowd. AUTHOR'S COLLECTION

Maynards above Rockwood also had camps located at good spots for hunting and fishing. Its lodge, cabins, and rooms on the Moose River, however, were designed for comfort. There were electric lights and running water, and some of the cabins had their own baths. Guests looked forward to sitting before the large stone fireplace, playing bridge, talking of expeditions into the forest, and listening to music.

West Outlet Camps, established in 1904, were advertised as "the largest most up-to-date camps in the state made of round logs." The cabins had wide piazzas and rocking chairs. A cabin with a private bath cost twenty-one dollars per week for two people. (There were no discounts for children over five or their nurses.) *Grandeur* was the word used in the brochure in describing the view from the grounds. Kineo's brow and the great cones of the Spencers rose across the coruscating expanse of the "king of mountain lakes." The dining room sat sixty guests at white-clothed tables. Canoe voyagers out on the rivers had biscuits baked in a reflector oven, but in the dining room the guests had to do with a menu that started with *consommé à la royal;* went on with broiled trout, mazarins of lobster, spring lamb, or sirloin of beef *au jus;* and ended with Spanish puffs with brandy sauce or vanilla ice cream with chocolate topping. There were croquet and tennis, or you could ride up the lake and play golf at Kineo's nine-hole course. A favorite

The Troutdale Camps on Lake Moxie, across the narrows from Troutdale Station. This getaway was first called the Mosquito Camps, until someone wisely decided that didn't make good business sense.

hike, named "round the horn" by one of the more notable and regular guests, took you four miles to Mike Marr's camps, where you could eat dinner and then walk an additional mile to the little station on the Somerset to catch a train for Rockwood. There a steamboat provided an evening run back to West Outlet.

At West Outlet the guides lived in a little village of tents between the main camp and the water tank. In a world very much concerned with social rank, the guide was an anomaly. His was a profession that gave elbow room to men who exemplified Jefferson's "natural aristocracy," be they white or Indian. There were many counterfeits, of course, like the young, ostentatious chap who bragged that he had guided the boxer Gene Tunney and who, when the crowd was appropriate, did cartwheels down the platform at Kineo Station. Once when drunk this fellow scared the baggage clerk half to death twirling a revolver and sending a round into the rafters. The real guides, however, were quiet men, made patient by tending to the needs of demanding people. Sitting around the campfire with keenly trained minds sharpened their capacity to select what was most significant in their own native idiom. There was a surprising charm in their manner for men who were so rugged and weather tanned. What transpired between such guides and appreciative employers was not so much egalitarianism as it was deep

During the last years when the railroad ran to Kineo, the Maine Central owned its own steamboat, the *Moosehead*. JOHN SYMONDS COLLECTION

Posing on an August day in 1910 are the maids at the railway's Rockwood Hotel. JOHN SYMONDS COLLECTION

respect between people who each had expertise within their own worlds. Over the years strong bonds of trust and esteem often grew between those who routinely came to the Maine woods and their guides. When the management of the Kineo House decided that it would be more decorous for the guides to live removed from the premises, the hotel lost much of its old-time clientele.

Kineo House was a five-story, pillared, porticoed, and towered transplant whose manicured lawns kept the woods at bay. When the Somerset arrived at Rockwood, the "Big House" was waiting to entertain five hundred guests in an atmosphere of Oriental rugs, private baths, linen, and crystal. To make sure that fire would not destroy the Big House, as it had all of its predecessors, a system of hydrants backed by a powerful steam pump had been installed, along with brick firewall within the hotel itself. Much of the required produce and meat was furnished by Deerhead Farm a short distance down the lake. At this farm a half acre of sweet peas was planted to provide flowers for the dining tables.

Those who ate too much could take one of the waiting elevators back to their rooms. There were bridle trails, a stable of horses, and hiking paths to special places such as Hardscrabble Point or the top of the felcite cliffs. From the

153

Maine Central Railroad Co. Terminal and Dock   Kineo Station, Maine

A postcard of the *Katahdin* and other steamboats alongside the railway
pier at Kineo Station on Moosehead Lake. ROBERT LORD COLLECTION

hotel's pier, parties bound for adventures in the wilderness left with canoes and
dunnage piled onto one of the many steamboats that plied the lake. For those
who wished to see wild townships spread out before them and return in time
for dinner, there was the climb up Kineo. And if you chose to go nowhere, there
always was the wide veranda, a reclining chair, and the view down the lake–the
islands dividing the waters, over it all an arch of sky resting on Squaw Mountain
and the peaks of Lily Bay.

It was an era of contrasts and rapid change ruled over by a society that
prized its technology and had become perhaps too conscious of itself. A few
years before the Somerset reached Moosehead, the best of its coaches had hanging oil lamps and potbellied stoves; now Pullman cars waited on the wharf at
Rockwood in a long, shining black line and with such names as the *Jasper* or
Albany lettered in gold leaf. One of the Coburn steamboats and the hotel's own
Olivette would be at the ramps. Baggage wagons loaded with trunks thumped
over the planks, while men in white suits and women in long dresses moved

154

toward the waiting porters at the car steps. There was excited talk from children and the bark of a dog being escorted toward the baggage car. Up front the air pump on the locomotive ceased to ca-chunk, and the brake lines were charged.

It was one A.M. when train number 118 reached Oakland and its cars were added to the Maine Central's Bar Harbor train. Passengers would be in their berths, except for the night owls playing cards or having a last cigar. By seven in the morning the Pullmans and parlor car were in Boston.

The people who came to the camps and the Big House lived in another world from those who labored on and along the Somerset. While the latter saved to take a yearly excursion, the former might pay twenty-five fares to reserve an entire coach for themselves and arrive at Kineo Station in style. It cost more to stay at the Kineo House for one night than a locomotive engineer earned in a week—and these men were at the top of the Somerset's pay scale, $2.40 per day.

The social world of Rockwood had become a complex web between the served and the serving. Yet at least among the old-guard summer people there existed a genuine level of pleasantry between themselves and the "natives." Station Agent Julian Estes and his wife Grace, for instance, were always welcome to use the boat of the president's son, John Coolidge, when he was not in Rockwood. (The younger Coolidge was engaged to the daughter of Connecticut's Governor Trumball, who had a camp on Spencer Bay.) There appears to have been an unspoken agreement as to social place, and only the nouveau riche insisted on labeling the boundaries.

People in Rockwood and at the Big House looked forward to the return of the notable regulars. Their arrivals gave color to the calendar. The yachting season began when Colonel Warring stepped off the train. The twelve-gauge cannon on the prow of the hotel's boat would be fired in salute; the colonel's own yacht, the *Ionita,* waited at the pier, her brass polished and the sun shining on the new varnish. As the yacht pulled away, Warring would stand and listen intently to the smooth hiss of the steam engine. The crew watched until he nodded his head in approval. There was pleasure in knowing that you owned the fastest steamboat on the lake. Everyone who had something to do with the *Ionita* was proud as well.

On warm afternoons while waiting to board the boats, summer folks stretched their legs walking the long platform at Kineo Station. For men the smart thing was a yachting cap—unless you were a true angler with your mind set on floating a dry fly in the pool below Canadian Falls. For women, unless they too had come to wet a fly, it was a white sunshade carried at just the right angle. A little twirl of the parasol was as seductive as the flickering of eyelash.

155

Racing rowed bateaux was just one of the summer sports enjoyed by patrons of the Kineo Hotel, visible in the background.
JOHN SYMONDS COLLECTION

(The status symbol of a suntan was unheard of. A woman hid from the sun and darted little smiles from under the fringe of her parasol.) These summer people would have been surprised to hear a railroader speak of Rockwood as the "hole." If it had been raining recently and if they had stepped off the platform, they would have discovered why.

In later years tons of cinders and gravel stabilized the track, and some grass took root, but when the Somerset first came to Rockwood there was mud. The ties were laid, the rails spiked down, and a prayer made to whatever rules the muck to dry things up. Boardwalks led from the station to Rockwood Hotel, and it was not wise to take a shortcut. Besides the mud, several other particulars of Rockwood Yard were worth knowing about.

Two parallel tracks ran out onto the pier. One was an extension of the main line, and the other ran past the freight house. (Both the passenger depot and the freight shed sat on the pier.) For some reason, certainly not brilliant, slips were put in on the western side of the pier; the freight track was laid at the edge of the openings without any attempt to board them over. It was an initiation for a greenhorn to swing off a boxcar and find himself in the lake. The sensation was more startling in spring and fall. One vacationer, supervising the unloading of his tent, slipped under the tracks and came up wedged between the wharf and a boat. His only remark on being pulled out was that his pipe had gone out. A good many of the "sports" were first-rate fellows.

There was another fact of which the transients were blissfully unaware: Water for the hotel, cottages, station, and engine plug came from a standpipe filled from the lake—and there wasn't a great deal of distance between this intake and the sewer discharge from the hotel. No one ever seemed to get sick at the Rockwood House, but the trainmen felt better about using springwater; a white rag tied to a branch marked a spring beside the track a mile below Kineo Station. Freight crews always stopped there and filled their water cans.

As much as the locals differed in means from the vacationers who came to Moosehead, they shared the same needs and interests. A Somerset man who spent time in Rockwood knew where he could get his hands on a canoe, and he had some idea where people were catching fish. Everyone used the store. For a small community, it was far larger than you might have suspected. A list of items needed for camping trips was printed in a folder for the convenience of the sports. For those heading out on a canoeing trip, the store furnished a kit that had about everything you needed, including an ax and butter at twenty cents a pound. Prices were a bit high, but a railroader's wife could find about anything she needed.

Behind the cottages that faced the tracks stood Rockwood Hall. Spirited dances were held here every Saturday night, and, when they'd become more common, movies were shown. But there was a lot to do without paying any admission. Watching the yacht races was fun, and so was ogling ladies or admiring their latest fashions as they descended the parlor car steps. Winter in Rockwood, of course, was a different story.

Julian Estes and his wife enjoyed the years they spent in Rockwood. When the agent in Bingham was getting sixty-four cents an hour, the station master at Kineo Station received nine cents more. His responsibilities were sizable and involved. The season of the year made little difference. In summer it was the vacation trade, baggage, larder, and piles of telegrams. Winter brought tons of wangan supplies and the army of loggers. Ticket sales could amount to $500 a day at a time when you could ride to Oakland for $2.50. There were special trains, excursions, and second sections of regular trains to keep in mind. Estes found it stimulating. He never knew when there would be some excitement.

The morning he found that the station safe had been blown was exciting enough. For Ralph Stone, the agent's helper in the freight shed, it was a morning of real anxiety. There had been a hundred dollars of his own money in the safe. It had taken a long time to save up that much cash. Estes and Stone collected the

At left, the wife of station agent Julian Estes. She is standing with friends by the awning on the wharf at Kineo Station. AUTHOR'S COLLECTION

scattered papers on the floor. Only one brown envelope was left in the safe. In it was Ralph's one hundred dollars.

The blowing of a safe was uncommon, but the taking of liquor got to be a regular problem. It might have been more feasible to ship spirits to Rockwood by the tankcar, but someone would have found a way to steal the entire car. So many liquor shipments were lost at Somerset Junction and at Rockwood that it became necessary to inspect the freight cars at Bingham and seal the doors. Ed Fogg–"Whistling Rufus," as he was called–got the job. Ed tunefully went on his rounds with a pocketful of lead seals and a sealing stamp that pressed out a flattened disk marked with a 62. When the freight got to Somerset Junction or Kineo Station with a seal broken, the sheriff was called.

On Estes's first day as station master at Kineo, a crate of very special whiskey shipped express from New York disappeared. Estes got a hot tip that the thieves had headed up the Moose River in a boat. The agent borrowed a boat and followed. When he passed an empty bottle with its distinctive label bobbing in the river, he knew that he was getting close. The thieves were in a congenial mood when the agent caught up with them and generously offered him a drink. Things quieted down for a while, until a keg of rum went missing. Estes questioned around and found out who had been drunk for some time. There were no hard feelings when the thief went to jail. Later he borrowed twenty dollars from the agent and paid him back.

The Esteses were a team. Agent Julian Estes was the first to give his wife credit for the clean and tidy look of the depot. Indeed, he was proud of his wife. She had a reputation as the best-dressed woman in Rockwood—and that included the out-of-state women getting on and off the train. Like her husband, Mrs. Estes looked back with happy memories on her work at Kineo Station. She went to work thinking, "Now, today so-and-so will be returning for the summer"—such was the regularity of the vacationers.

John King, a close adviser to Teddy Roosevelt, spent his summers in Rockwood. Mrs. Estes took a telegram to him one afternoon. It was an urgent summons for him to return to the melee of politics. King shook his head sadly when the agent's wife asked him if the Bull Moose Party had a chance that fall.

Many other notable people came and went as well. Holman Day wrote one of his books while staying at the West Outlet Camps. A cartoonist for the New York papers also stayed at the Outlet. He brought his drawings to the station, let Mrs. Estes have a peek, and then made sure they got off by express mail.

One of the two large boys' camps close to Rockwood was Whooper's Wildwood establishment. Connected to Colgate, the camp managed to have exceptional guest speakers. Mrs. Estes had been reading *Wild Animals I Have Known,* and the name "Ernest Thompson Seton" in a telegram caught her attention. Whooper promised to introduce her to Seton when he came to lecture. One afternoon a white-haired gentleman came and sat on a baggage wagon and talked with Mrs. Estes. Later she found that she had spent a pleasant half hour with the famous writer and naturalist.

In fall, near the end of the vacation season, Mrs. Estes looked forward to the arrival of the William Tell Club. They came by special train ready to hunt and above all have a good time at their camp on Spencer Bay. Mrs. Estes's father-in-law belonged to this club. The membership was fairly exclusive. It included the two bearded Ricker brothers of Poland Spring fame; Arthur Staples, a first-rate journalist and editor of the *Lewiston Journal;* Dan Webster, an official for American Express; and the owners of the Lewiston woolen mills. Having spent their holiday, the club members returned to Rockwood, where they gave a dance for the public. Mrs. Estes decorated the hall. One year she spent a lot of time hanging apples pierced with arrows only to find that the club wasn't named for that William Tell. No matter—the dance was a grand affair. The women even received a gift of costume jewelry.

The Boston Company of Ancient and Honorable Artillery also came to Rockwood in a special train as long as the organization's name. It was an invasion without cannon of hale and hearty souls. With banners and flags flying they lined up on the station platform, anticipating their once-a-year blowout.

The official and private cars arrived much more quietly but with regal varnish and gold leaf. These cars were set off on track number 1; this was fairly close to the hotel and store, and offered hook-ups for water and electricity. Once the awnings were in place, these cars became opulent homes rivaling the best accommodations at the Big House. The Maine Central's official cars, numbers 500 and 600, were often there, along with Lucius Tuttle's car from the Boston & Maine. Occasionally an official car from another more distant road occupied track 1. Julian Estes was once offered a job by an official of an Iowa railroad. Julian admitted that it was actually his wife who was wanted. The official had been impressed with the waxed floors and clean toilets at the station.

Most quiet of all in their coming were the private cars, which kept their anonymity. Rockwood seemed far enough removed from scandal to be a hideaway. Still, you could tell when there was a party in the making even before these private cars arrived. Several girls would get off the train, adding their attractiveness to cosmopolitan Rockwood in the summertime.

In season, deer hunters kept the railroad busy. These whitetails are tagged and ready to be loaded into the baggage car at Kineo Station.
AUTHOR'S COLLECTION

Nights eventually became chilly and days cool, as if the air had suddenly grown too clear and rarefied for the sun to heat. Fall came, and Maine burned with color yet was not consumed (at least for a few weeks). Every stream and lake became a watercolor copy of the brilliance along their banks and the autumn blue of the sky. If you could have but one ride on the Somerset from Oakland to Moosehead, fall would be the season to choose. Then, standing on the rear platform, you could watch a world of scarlets and oranges, yellows and softwood greens flowing behind. Fallen leaves, fragments of color, would swirl and settle once again.

A few weeks more, a night of wind and rain, and all would be changed. The hunters came with the falling of the leaves and the first snow on the mountaintops. At Kineo Station baggage wagons were soon loaded with deer stacked like cordwood to be shipped express to Boston or New York or Philadelphia—fifty or more every Saturday morning. And then the sporting season was over for another year. The four crack passenger trains per day would be taken off, leaving just the old regular coaches to transport the loggers and the village inhabitants.

Before the big lake finally froze, the Coburn boats were drawn up on the shore at Greenville Junction, the yachts were tucked in, and winter inexorably came. Tote teams crossing the ice from Rockwood to Kineo would find their way in a world of blowing snow by following the row of fir trees set up and frozen in the ice. For seven months Rockwood would be no place for yachting caps and white sunshades.

Chapter Thirteen

TAIL MARKERS

CHANCES ARE THAT NO railroad had more delays due to hotboxes on their freight trains than did the Somerset. It is also likely that no one at the Oakland office was particularly concerned that most of these occurred beside well-known fishing holes. Fresh trout frying on the buggy stove at the end of a long day's run was an inexpensive employee fringe benefit.

The management went fishing as well. George Foster, who became the Somerset's superintendent following William Ayer, got up one morning with the urge to go get some trout. There didn't seem to be anything too pressing on his platter, so George took the train north. At North Anson the red order board was up and Lester Williams, the station agent, on the platform with a telegram for George. It was a summons from Morris MacDonald, president of the Maine Central. He wanted to see Foster in Portland immediately. Foster tried to think of a good excuse, but there wasn't any. Of more immediate importance, there also wasn't a southbound train that would connect with the next Portland train passing through Oakland.

The men on the Somerset called Foster "satchel ass" when he wasn't around, but here was a fellow railroader in trouble. Williams had a REO car and he offered it. Foster jumped at a ray of hope.

"Now," said Foster, using one of his favorite expressions, "if we go like a goose shitting, we may make it to Oakland in time to catch that train."

They started in a cloud of dust, and Lester kept the REO humping until the gas line broke. The agent got out his tire tape and yellow soap–two things it didn't pay to be without–while Foster paced around the car looking dejected and distracted in turns. As they wheeled into Oakland Yard, the Portland train was just disappearing toward a waiting railroad president. Lester never did get paid for his gas, nor learn just what excuse Foster finally cooked up.

In 1911 the Maine Central assumed the managerial reins and began pulling at the bit. There was an immediate impact on the employees working at the Somerset's home base. The Oakland shops were closed. Then came the new rules–all 982 of them, many of which had to be crammed into your head before examination time. The new "brass" did not call men by their first names, and when Morris MacDonald came north, he rode in his own private car. On one trip to Rockwood he gave orders to have his car run into the engine house, where its water tanks could be filled. Crossing the turntable, the switching crew stopped the process and were discussing whether the top of the car would clear the smoke jacks inside the engine house when MacDonald came striding up. Impatiently he motioned the engineer to continue. The train crew was disappointed when the cartop cleared.

The takeover did not alter services. What the public saw was business as usual. There were even some improvements. Buildings got a new coat of paint, and Deadwater got a new station with hard pine sheathing. The road remained far enough removed to allow for small irregularities–for instance, freight crews still picked up the minister from Bingham after leaving him beside the track to fish Baker Stream or the East Branch below Indian Pond. Still, many felt that the annexation to the larger road was the beginning of the end for rail service along the upper Kennebec.

On March 11, 1929, the dissolution of the Somerset Railway was officially declared. To use an old phrase, those who had put so much into winning a railroad for their communities must have turned in their graves. However, for the relatively few now in control, the dissolution was a legal technicality. The tracks were still there, and the trains continued to run. Other developments seemed more worth pondering. How much was left of the big timber north of Deadwater? What changes was the automobile making in the vacation business that had brought hotels like the Kineo House such financial success? What would trucks, which had the advantage of using the public roads, do to railroad freight, express, and the carrying of the mails? And after the fall of 1929, one question transcended all others: Would the country survive the Great Depression?

Amid the dismal conditions and the national misery, Bingham and Moscow were experiencing a boom of sorts. The Central Maine Power Company had chosen a site in Moscow for its new dam and power station. It would be the largest of its kind in the East. The village of Moscow became a town of small houses, and to the old music of the Kennebec was added a cacophony of steam shovels, pneumatic drills, and cement mixers. The railroad built several miles of spur from Bingham Yard up a tremendous fill to the site.

Business on the Somerset Branch may not have been prosperous, but operations were still in the black. For example, the Augusta Lumber Company still had a busy sawmill at Deadwater. Pearl Woodard had kept records of the earnings and expenditures along the branch. These figures seemed to substantiate his own conviction that passenger traffic deserved at least a mixed train daily. Still, the rumors grew that the line above Bingham would be abandoned and that all passenger service on the branch was to be taken off. To Pearl and many other railroaders, it looked as if such branch lines were being closed and their equipment and properties sold by larger conglomerates to supplement their own failing revenues.

It was frustrating. One official sent to observe and evaluate the Somerset Branch spent all his time at Moosehead. A Maine Central officer did take a look at Pearl's records. He was impressed, especially with the earnings from excursion trains, but he doubted that the big boys would be. Shortly afterward, the fares on all excursions went up. Trains that had been crowded to the steps became private runs for the conductors and their brakemen. Such tactics were transparent.

In 1932 the last regular passenger train ran from Bingham to Oakland. For a year-and-a-half longer, people in Bingham could still take the train at Bingham Heights; then on July 22, 1933, the last passenger train left Kineo Station for Oakland. The last regular freight rumbled south down the grade from Deadwater just six days later.

The rails from Bingham to Rockwood remained for another three years. Their once silver-smooth surfaces became red with rust. Several sporting camps remodeled automobiles by adding flanged wheels, then used them to transport guests from Moxie and Bingham to their establishments on the rails. One of these "jetneys" making a trip up the grade from Bingham to Lake Austin met a rare extra freight running south from Deadwater. One woman was seriously injured in this last collision on the Kineo Branch.

On October 13, 1936, crews began taking up the track from Austin Junction northward. The rail was sold as junk metal to a buyer in Japan. Freight service to Bingham continued until 1975. No one seems to have noted the date that the last train crossed the field below Bingham and followed the riverside track to Solon. North Anson became the railhead again for a while, until there was another amputation. Now the track ends in a pile of gravel and bushes just north of Madison's main street.

The Somerset had existed for fewer years than a man may hope to live—one short of three-score years and ten from first charter to the date of dissolution. It seems incredible that so much work and living, so many changes, schemes, and expectations, could have crowded into so small a world and so few years.

The Somerset was an aggregate of lives and enterprises. Its two rails threaded a valley of farms and forests. They stitched together a human story lived out between an older way of life and an accelerating age.

One man, remembering, told me he recalled working for the Somerset less as a job than as a challenge. It seemed an adventure rather than just a livelihood.

Some years ago Reed Hilton went back to the site of the Somerset's shops in Oakland. He wrote me:

"Was over to Oakland this P.M. and walked down to the old shop area. It will be fifty-one years since I left, and I had the foolish thought that I would like to go down. Those years have erased the buildings and a lot of other things connected with the little pike, but they can't take away the memories or the fact that once one worked with a group of men who would be hard to find these days. I stood for a moment on the rim of the old turntable. All those fellows long gone seemed to be tramping across the path toward the machine shop. I remember them as a group who never complained and done an honest day's work, had their horseplay and were first to give in case of need.

"Then the thoughts came in a tumble all unexpected: I wondered what had happened to that little dark-haired June and her smaller sister? They were always at the window of the section house at Bakers to wave and watch us pass. And I wondered to myself: If one stood amidst Deadwater's wind and drifting snow, might one hear again a screech owl answer the chime of old number 22 whistling at the upper switch?"

PART IV

Appendices

The old engine *Somerset*, owned by Colonel Ayer, pulls a fine,
well-decorated coach. Taken circa 1875 at Oakland, this photograph
shows A. W. Leonard's store in the background.

Appendix

MOTIVE POWER AND ROLLING STOCK

Over the years the Somerset had a remarkable collection of locomotives, some shiny new from the builders, others destined for the junk pile. I am indebted to R. F. Dole for his meticulous research on Somerset locomotives. However, it is not possible to produce an exact roster of Somerset motive power. Secondhand engines came and went, sometimes lasting no more than a couple of years. A letter I found in the Maine Central archives mentioned that the Somerset was a good place to unload old locomotives. Despite this reputation as an old loco-motives' home, the Somerset managed to do some "deaconing" of its own. In 1891 it bought a Manchester locomotive for $750 and made $100 profit when it sold the engine to the Decker Lumber Company for $850 eight years later.

Superintendent Bill Ayer got old Cap Crowell, the railroad's mechanical genius, to look over a secondhand locomotive he was thinking of buying. Cap limped around on his game leg, peering in at the links. He unbolted the smoke arch door and scrutinized the petticoat pipe and flues. Finally, he inspected the piping in the cab.

"Well, what do you think?" Bill asked.

Cap looked down from the cab window, wiping his hands on a wad of waste. "I'd say she has all the ancient improvements," he answered.

Even the first locomotive to run on Somerset rails had seen her better days. She was named the *General Veazie* and was on loan from the Maine Central. Built by the Kerk Company and originally named the *Saint Louis,* this engine had first run on the European & North American Railroad before being bought by the Maine Central. The *Veazie* huffed and wheezed her way from Oakland to the railhead at Martin Stream hauling rail and ties until the Somerset got an engine of its own. This locomotive, too, had been around, having been used on the Portland, Saco & Portsmouth Railroad as well as on the Eastern Railroad. She began her new life appropriately renamed the *Somerset*. Built by the Hinkley Locomotive Works, she was an "American" type (four pony wheels and four drivers). She had what was called a cabbage stack, which flared out like a funnel–the design typically seen on wood-burning engines. Her boiler was sleek, the large oil headlamp projected out above her cowcatcher, the fenders over the spoked driving wheels were trimmed in gold, and the cross-head pumps and domes were brass. She was still beautiful.

In 1875 the railroad bought a second locomotive to spell the hard-worked *Somerset*. The *Old Point* was a Maine-born engine built in 1869, the 150th locomotive to roll out of the Portland Company's shops. Having been rebuilt in the Eastern Railroad's shops before arriving in Oakland, this locomotive no longer wore the builder's plate with its "Portland star," but she retained the fine lines of the Portland locomotives.

The *Somerset* finally wore out and was replaced with another Hinkley locomotive. She assumed the numerical distinction of 1 but was named the *Caratunk*. Starting with the *Caratunk* and ending with the *Messalonskee* as number 7, there were the *Old Point*, the *Norridgewock*, the *Carrabassett*, the *Moxie*, the *Bombazeen*, and finally the *Messalonskee*. Each engine was also numbered. The *Old Point* was number 2, the *Norridgewock* number 3, and so on. Over the years more than one

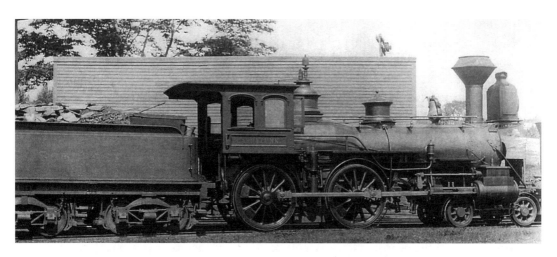

Replacing the old *Somerset*, the *Caratunk* become engine No. 1.
She was built by Hinkley in 1869.

ROBERT LORD COLLECTION

engine took its turn bearing these names and numbers. There appears to have been two number 2s at the same time, but the older engine with this number was confined to yard work and nicknamed "Black Dinah."

Greatest in longevity among these early engines was the *Bombazeen,* old number 6. She was Cap Crowell's favorite; the "Old Lady," he called her. She even got in on building the extension above Bingham, hauling rail and ties to the railhead. The engine had a peculiarity in her Stevenson valve linkage that allowed her to stop on center. (Ordinarily, a locomotive can't stop on center unless one cylinder is not working.) Cap would crawl under the engine, give a couple of affectionate raps with a ball-peen hammer, and get back into the cab. The Old Lady would be ready to go on cutting her strokes like a pocket watch.

The last of the named engines was the *Messalonskee.* The name filled the full width of her cab below the side windows. Brand new and built by Baldwin to William Ayer's specifications, the *Messalonskee* cost ten thousand dollars. Her pop valve was set for 180 pounds, an increase of 35 pounds of boiler pressure over locomotives that had earlier steamed along the banks of the upper Kennebec. The *Messalonskee* was Engineer Ed Magoon's favorite on the run from Oakland to Kineo Station. She could handle a baggage car, a smoking car, and a Pullman on the mountain, and take another Pullman by dropping five miles off her running

Another fine-looking traditional engine, this is No. 2, the *Old Point.*
She is recorded as having been built by the Portland Company and
certainly has the lines for which that firm was known.
That's the mechanic shop at Oakland in the background.
AUTHOR'S COLLECTION

speed. When the Maine Central took over, the *Messalonskee* became the new owner's number 85. In 1924 she was left on a siding to rust and wait for the flare of the cutting torch. Everywhere progress was racing ahead at a terrific cost.

The locomotives' names belonged to the proud Indian heritage of the valley. *Caratunk* was the Abenaki name for that portion of the Kennebec above the great falls at Solon. Long before the Somerset pushed its rails northward, that designation had been narrowed to the falls themselves. Norridgewock—a name dreadful to the early English settlers—was the site of the principal Abenaki village at Old Point. Carrabassett was an old chief and defender of the tribe who died at the gate of that Indian town the day it was captured and burned by the colonists. Bombazeen (or Bombazee) also lost his life that day. He had spotted the English coming up the river and was on his way with a warning when he was intercepted and shot. *Moxie* seems to be an old Indian title for an elected chief, but its exact meaning has been lost along with the legend that links this honored title to a mountain north of Deadwater. *Messalonskee* whispers the beauty of that lake at the head of which the Somerset's tracks began. Up and down the banks of that great river, the railroad's engines, in their dramatic coming and going, bore the names of a people who silently traveled this way long before.

By 1907 the practice of naming locomotives had been lost in the race for prosaic efficiency. When the railway bought two new Manchester locomotives, it simply numbered them 10 and 12. These were state-of-the-art passenger engines (4-4-0s). They carried 180 pounds of pressure, were mounted on sixty-three-inch drivers, and had a price tag of $10,271 each. The high wagontops over the rear of the boilers, the straight shotgun stacks, and the unadorned domes were all utility. Gone were the ornate bell supports turned in brass, the long overhang of the cab roof, and the scrollwork under the headlamp brace. The classic lines of the old *Somerset* or the *Caratunk* were gone, but these new locomotives could keep their schedules with four hundred tons of baggage and passenger cars behind them. They survived the Somerset, by the way, and became the Maine Central numbers 86 and 87. Finally they ended up belonging to a road in Vermont.

Handling freight on the grades above Bingham called for something bigger. The next additions to the Somerset's motive power were two ten-wheelers (four pony wheels and six driving wheels) newly made at the Baldwin locomotive shops. Designated numbers 22 and 23, they were the pride of the Somerset's motive power. As is true of all freight engines, the drivers were smaller than those found on passenger engines. (Big-diameter drivers for speed, smaller for power.) Fifty-four inches in diameter, they made the engines seem to crouch over the rails. They were powered by cylinders eighteen inches in bore

A classic beauty, Somerset No. 4 was named the *Carrabassett*.
Her builder is unknown.
AUTHOR'S COLLECTION

Somerset No. 12 was an example of the new 4–4–0 passenger engines
acquired by the railroad when it extended the line to Moosehead Lake.
Built in 1907 by Manchester, she had five-foot-three-inch drivers and
carried 180 pounds of steam pressure.
AUTHOR'S COLLECTION

and twenty-four inches in stroke. These new locomotives were ten feet longer than the biggest engines on the road. New additions had to be tacked onto the engine houses, and the turntables extended. The latter was no small job. It may have been at this time that the walls of the turntable pits were constructed of poured concrete.

In November 1875 John Ayer, Esquire, president of the railroad, received the following note: "My engine [sawing machine] and crew are laying in Hallowell and if you would like to have me saw that wood again at Norridgewock, please let me know tomorrow."

This was a message from the era when the Somerset was burning wood in the fireboxes of its locomotives. Up until the late 1890s, long wood sheds were a

The new "ten-wheelers" (an engine designated the 4–6–0) were the pride of the Somerset Railroad. Bought new from the Baldwin Locomotive Works, they each had a tractive effort of 21,600 pounds, weighed 180,000 pounds, and carried 12,000 pounds (six tons) of coal and 3,800 gallons of water. Shown here is Somerset No. 21 after she had been renamed **Maine Central 107.** AUTHOR'S COLLECTION

prominent feature in every railroad yard along the Somerset. Each fall these sheds were crammed full of two-foot sticks. Engines and their tenders would come alongside the sheds to "wood up." Burning wood meant sparks, and the stacks of locomotives went through an evolution of shapes in an effort to control the potential threat to the property and countryside along the tracks. The sight of a wood burner after dark throwing sparks at the sky was a reason for concern. Still, only after the railway switched to burning coal was it charged with setting serious forest fires.

People in villages such as Deadwater and Moxie had a right to be concerned about forest fires. They were surrounded with the slash left from logging operations. The summer directly following the Somerset's extension to Moosehead was very dry. The agent at Deadwater kept track of the water level in Austin Flowage. Each day the dead trees in the flowage showed a brown ring left by the dropping water level. No one in the woods above Bingham needed to be reminded that a forest fire is a terrifying destroyer that burns both beneath the ground and in the treetops, where it travels far faster than any high-wheeled locomotive.

The fires came. At Indian Pond the conflagration was blamed on the sparks from one of the Somerset's engines. Arthur Tupper, the engineer on the westbound, first spotted the fire. It was small then. Adrian Robinson, the brakeman on the same train, thought that the crew could have put it out with brooms. They dropped a fire card warning the first section crew they passed. Train number 15, which was on the siding at Indian Pond, was given orders to get through the fire as soon as possible and head for Rockwood. The fire was no longer small when number 15 entered the pall of smoke. Burning twigs swirled into the engine cab, while the heat seared the varnish on both sides of the coaches. It was a near thing. As the fire raged on, the heat expanded the rails until they twisted like snakes and the cedar ties blazed.

Historian Mary Calvert has recorded a wonderful story of an excursion train heading for Rockwood that encountered small fires on both sides of the track south of Moxie Pond. While the crew went ahead to inspect the track, the Bingham band—which was along for the outing—struck up a Sousa march. Possibly this adventure was connected with one of the "Dimmick fires." If so, the train was fortunate. It is reported that the first Dimmick fire burned the land black, and the second consumed the very earth. Deadwater was spared, but a fire close by left its scorching mark in the charred trunks of a wasted woodland. There seems no evidence that the railroad was responsible for the latter fires.

The railway's response to the threat of sparks was to experiment with burning oil in its locomotives. Cap Crowell was in a black mood when spring came each year–time to convert from coal. An oil tank was set into the tender, lines connected, atomizers and nozzles installed, and some changes made in the flues. The problem was that no two engines demanded the same settings. There was more guess and b'gosh than technology in getting an oil burner to function properly.

The oil-fired engines were hotter than hell without water to ride in. They could be hotter than that if the fireman didn't shut down the oil feed and turn on the blower when the engineer stopped working steam. Many a fireman lost his whiskers in a backfire. To keep the flues clean, the fireman would toss a shovelful of fine sand through the fire door. Brakemen always claimed that this was done only when they were walking the tops of the cars and exposed to the sandblasting.

Bulk fuels were not classified when the Somerset did its experimenting. The oil used was close to what would now be graded number four bunker fuel. It had to be warm to flow properly. It arrived in the old-style wooden tankcars belonging to the Union Tank Company. At first the tender's tanks were filled directly from these cars with a single-action steam pump fed from the locomotive boiler. When this practice proved too slow, the railway set up storage tanks and oil spouts at Oakland and Rockwood.

The trials and tribulations of burning oil didn't last many seasons. When the project was abandoned, somebody dumped what was left in the Rockwood storage tank into Moosehead. That night Leon Greely paddled his girlfriend over to the dance at the Big House. Leon had on white pants, his girl a white frock. They both agreed that the water felt greasy, but Leon's girl kept trailing her fingers in the water and Leon wiping his hand on his pants. They were a harlequin of black crude and white cloth when they stepped into the lights of the dance hall. A crew from the Somerset spent a lot of time that summer cleaning the hulls of pleasure craft, but of course that didn't much help Leon or his girlfriend.

It was the consumption figures that finally convinced the railway to go back to coal. Locomotives numbers 10 and 12, when coupled with regular passenger trains, averaged 297 gallons on a run from Oakland to Kineo. The freight engines with five hundred tons of train behind them burned closer to 350 gallons per trip.

Whether a railroad burns wood, coal, or oil, though, it runs on lubricants–oil and grease for the journals, the cross heads, and the eccentrics. The need was constant. On a downgrade–such as the one at Bombazee Rips or from Embden

Another of the railroad's ten-wheelers, this is Somerset No. 9, which was subsequently renumbered Somerset No. 20 and later became Maine Central No. 106. Perhaps the photographer wanted to emphasize how these engines towered over the Somerset's earlier motive power.

to Caratunk Falls—and while the engineer was not working steam, the fireman would fill the oil cups located over the boiler and in front of the steam turret. This done, he closed the cups and turned on the steam, which blew the oil into the cylinders. Before the Somerset was done, new automatic oilers did the same job one drop at a time. There were six hundred drops of oil to a pint of cylinder oil, as any good engineer could have told you. Oil consumption was watched carefully. The enginemen who used too much or too little got to visit with the Somerset's superintendent.

Signal oil cost the most. In the old days sperm oil was used in the headlights, signal lanterns, and lamps hung in the coaches. There was a cask left when the Oakland shops closed. The contents were carefully divided among the members of the shop crew as if they were all participating in an anointing of the past and the passing.

The first Somerset locomotives wore fancy decorations, and so did the coaches they pulled. The railroad bought its first coach in 1874—a new one, but there is no record as to the builder. Patten Car Works in Bath, Maine, built many early coaches for the Maine Central; it may have built the Somerset's first passenger car. These old cars were mounted on high-pedestal trucks, which made them stand tall on the track. The carpenters who built them had cabinetmaking abilities, and their creations were rich in paneling, moldings, and gold leaf inside and out. Along the rooftop ran a central clerestory filled with colored glass.

One of these old Somerset coaches sat on the wheel track in back of the Oakland shops for several years until it was hauled away and burned for scrap. The paint was badly faded and cracked, but enough pigment remained to show why the old coaches were nicknamed "circus wagons." The car had been a dark red, while the arching moldings over the narrow windows and along the sides were yellow. The fascia board under the roof's edge was also a golden yellow, with SOMERSET RAILROAD painted in dark brown letters. Step braces, railings, and smoke jacks were black, while the step risers were bright red. At the center of the car's side, just under the windows, was an oval shield carved with a white bird soaring and framed by the name of the road in green.

The colored glass used in the clerestory and in the toilet of those coaches repaired and rebuilt in the car shop at Oakland was bought from the Laconia Car Works in New Hampshire—pebbled red and green, respectively. Alternate windows in the clerestory were hinged and could be let down for ventilation. These openings were covered with screens; still, soot and coal smoke from the engine filtered in.

The oil lamps in these coaches gave a soft light that seemed to melt into the paneling. Hanging from the ceiling, a pair of lamps was supported in an inverted T of brass, with the lamp fonts inserted in circular brackets at each end of the crossbar. The fonts were brass as well, and each held a pint of sperm oil. Lamp chimneys ran up through enameled shades that reflected light downward and cast large shadows on the ceiling above. Whoever designed the coach lamps forgot to arrange a way to lift the lamp chimneys off the fonts. When it came time to light up, a trainman had to stand spread-legged on the chair arms to lift the chimney with one hand while the other held a burning match. A sudden lurch could land him in the lap of a passenger—which, at best, would be embarrassing.

White wood and mahogany were used for interior paneling. The ceiling paneling started out lighter in color than the walls, but darkened over the years with smoke from the coach stove and engine. Later the whole effect was desecrated by advertising cards placed in the crown along the ceiling.

The old Somerset coach stored at the Oakland shops had seats upholstered with a reddish material. The plush had disappeared with use. Leather was also used as a seat covering in some of the Somerset's cars, especially in the combination smoking-baggage cars. The back of each coach seat was reversible so that you could sit facing forward no matter which way the car was being hauled.

It is significant that such fancy coaches were used when many of the riders felt they owned a bit of the railroad. These cars were also the product of an era in which beauty had not become synonymous with utility. If something was worth building, it deserved to be elegant.

When the Maine Central took over, the Somerset had fifteen coaches, nine baggage cars, twelve combination cars, forty-eight forty-ton boxcars (twenty of which had been built by the Portland Company), forty-one log bunks, thirteen Roger ballast cars, nine general-service cars, six plows (including four of the notorious wedges), and twenty-one pumpcars for the section crews.

Appendix

GLOSSARY OF TERMS

4-4-0 *See* **Locomotive Types**.

4-6-0 *See* **Locomotive Types**.

Boomcar *See* **Donkey Crane**.

Brake Club A short, solid stick used in the old days as a lever to tighten hand brakes on railroad cars.

Buggy One of the many names for the caboose from which the crew on the rear of a train kept watch on the other cars and in which the crew slept and cooked meals.

Bunkcar A railroad car fitted to provide sleeping quarters for train and work crews.

Cabbage Stack An early shape of locomotive stack with flaring sides designed to increase draft and control the emission of sparks.

Calk Studded Boots Calks were metal cleats that could be screwed into the soles of boots to provide sure footing when walking or riding logs. A popular calk was invented and manufactured by Amon Baker of Bingham, Maine.

Carhouse A shed to house passenger cars when not in use.

Commanding Grade The steepest grade in a section of track. It determines the weight of trains that can be hauled.

Cookcar A railroad car remodeled to provide a facility for feeding work crews.

Coupling The mechanism by which rail cars are connected together or to the locomotive to form the train. Over the years, couplings improved from hand-manipulated to automatic devices *(see diagram).*

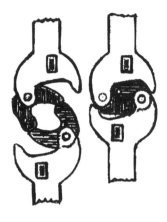

Cross Head The sliding link between the piston rod and the main rod that delivered power to the driving wheels.

Donkey Crane A crane consisting of a short boom and mast used to lift small loads. Mounted on a flatcar, it was called a boomcar *(see sketch).*

Coupling.

Donkey Engine On the Somerset, this was a steam engine with a vertical boiler used to power a crane.

Doubling The practice of dividing a train so that each half could be pulled separately up a steep grade.

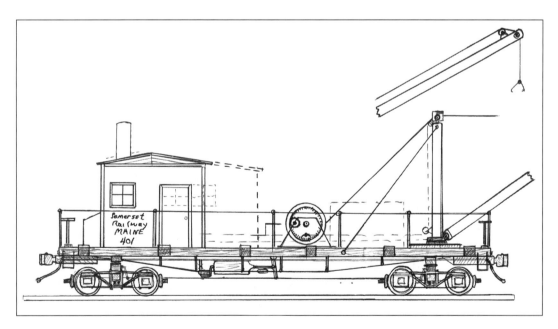

This sketch of Somerset's home-made boomcar was done from memory by
Reed Hilton, a long-time Somerset employee.

Double Heading Using two locomotives to pull a train.

Engine House Building used to shelter locomotives when not in use (*See also:* **Roundhouse**).

Fire Card A piece of cardboard upon which a train crew wrote the location of a fire spotted along the track. These cards were then passed to the first section crew encountered.

Fire Box The chamber that contains the fire aboard a steam locomotive. The fire box, along with the part of the boiler that encases it, protrudes into the locomotive cab.

Flanger A piece of equipment with a plow blade designed to clear snow from around the rails.

Flatcar A railroad car having a flat bed without sides, although stakes along the sides of the car are often used to secure a load. Platform car was an older descriptive term for such a car.

Handcar *See* **Pumpcar**.

Headworks A raft with a capstan and anchor used to tow booms of logs and pulp across lakes.

High Ball A signal giving a train crew permission to get underway. It was derived from the old signals that employed actual balls hoisted up a mast to give the go-ahead signal.

Hotbox The **journal**s *(which see)* on railroad cars' wheels were packed with lubricant-saturated **waste** *(which see)*. If the journals overheated, this waste could ignite.

Journal The ends of the wheel axles where the weight of a railroad car or locomotive is placed. It consists of a bearing and a means of lubrication. The entire mechanism is placed in a journal box.

Locomotive Types Locomotives are classified by the total number of wheels they have. In addition there is often a name attached. The classification 4-4-0 indicates that there are four smaller wheels–two on each side–before the four much larger drive wheels. In this example, there are no other wheels following the drive wheels. The wheel arrangement looks like this: o o O O (engine facing left). This type of locomotive is also called an American. A 4-6-0 has the following wheel arrangement: o o O O O, and is often spoken of as a ten-wheeler. Another locomotive type that appeared on the Somerset was 2-6-0, with a wheel arrangement of o O O O. These were called moguls.

Log Bunk A four-wheeled truck and bolster used to transport logs. The logs formed their own car when chained to a log bunk at each end.

Signal Board A signal semaphore mounted on a mast above a station roof. It combined both lights and two armlike boards that could be raised or lowered from within the station. The red signal board controlled east-bound trains and the white board controlled west-bound trains.

Pilot The plowlike contrivance at the very front of a locomotive, positioned just above the rails of the track. On early locomotives these "cowcatchers" were elaborate and prominent.

Pilot Wheels The smaller wheels supporting the front of a locomotive. Also called the locomotive truck wheels.

Platform Car *See* **Flatcar**.

Pumpcar Otherwise known as a hand-car. A light, four-wheeled vehicle typically used by track crews. It had a double-ended pump handle that allowed two men to furnish the motive power *(see sketch)*.

Pumpcar.

Rackcar A railroad car specially built to carry pulpwood.

Rerail A steel block designed to guide a wheel back onto a rail.

Roundhouse A building for housing locomotives. Usually facing a **turntable** *(which see)*, these houses were constructed over radiating tracks and thus were semi-circular in layout *(see diagram on next page)*.

Saloon Brake A passenger car hand brake–saloon car being an old name for a particular design of passenger car.

Smoke Jack   As used in this text, the term refers to the chimneys that collected and vented the locomotive smoke in a roundhouse.

Stevenson Valve Gear   One of the earliest linkages used to control the proper sequencing of the valves admitting steam into a locomotive's cylinders. A feature of this linkage was the forklike tines that engaged the valve rods.

Stop On Center   Stopping a locomotive in such a way that the position of the valve gear prevents starting again. Ordinarily, this can only happen when one of the locomotive's two cylinders is not operating.

Stumpage   An agreed-upon price per cord or other count paid to the landowner by the cutter.

Tankcar   A railroad car designed for transporting liquids.

Ten Wheelers   *See* **Locomotive Types**.

Toolcar   A railroad car used to carry the tools and equipment needed for working on wrecks or for other jobs along the track.

Torpedo   A small device placed on the rail, the torpedo would explode when run over, thus giving a warning signal to the train crew.

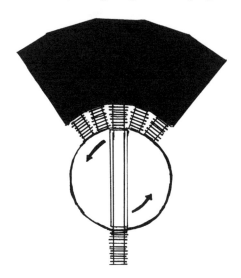

Roundhouse and turntable.

Turntable   A contrivance for turning engines and other railroad equipment. These tables were so well pivoted that the train crews were able to turn an engine by hand with push bars. Later turntables were powered by small engines using steam from the locomotives *(see diagram)*.

Waste   Cotton fiber left from the weaving process and used as a wipe for machinery of all sorts.

Wayfreight   Freight delivered and collected along the line, often composed of smaller and sundry items.

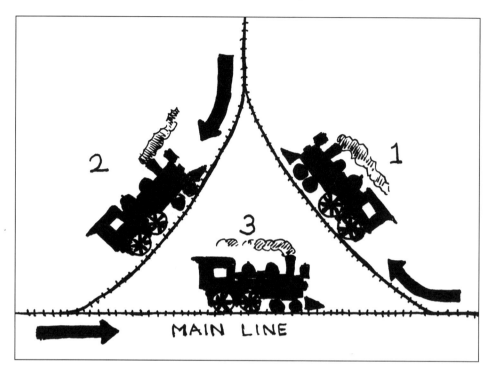

Diagram of a Y.

Y An arrangement of track that allows the turning around of locomotives and other railroad equipment *(see diagram).*

Appendix

INDEX